Business Cycles
Theories and Numerical Simulation

AF765667

DYNAMISCHE WIRTSCHAFTSTHEORIE

Herausgegeben von
Peter Flaschel und Michael Krüger

Band 12

PETER LANG
Frankfurt am Main · Bern · New York · Paris

Nobuo Okishio (ed.)

Business Cycles

Theories and Numerical Simulation

PETER LANG
Frankfurt am Main · Bern · New York · Paris

Die Deutsche Bibliothek - CIP-Einheitsaufnahme

Business cycles : theories and numerical simulation / Nobuo Okishio (ed.). - Frankfurt am Main ; Bern ; New York ; Paris : Lang, 1992
(Dynamische Wirtschaftstheorie ; Bd. 12)
ISBN 3-631-44410-9

NE: Okishio, Nobuo [Hrsg.]; GT

ISSN 0930-2174
ISBN 3-631-44410-9

© Verlag Peter Lang GmbH, Frankfurt am Main 1992
Alle Rechte vorbehalten.

Das Werk einschließlich aller seiner Teile ist urheberrechtlich geschützt. Jede Verwertung außerhalb der engen Grenzen des Urheberrechtsgesetzes ist ohne Zustimmung des Verlages unzulässig und strafbar. Das gilt insbesondere für Vervielfältigungen, Übersetzungen, Mikroverfilmungen und die Einspeicherung und Verarbeitung in elektronischen Systemen.

Preface

The purposes of this book are as follows :

1. The occurrence of business cycles are closely connected with the essential features of a capitalist economy. The first aim of this book is to clarify this relationship.
2. To recount the history of business cycles in Japan and some other leading capitalist economies during the postwar period. We hope readers find it useful to review the actual economic movements.
3. To survey a variety of business cycle theories in both the Marxian and Orthodox economic traditions.
4. To construct a simple mathematical model and demonstrate the relationships between economic variables. We hope this helps readers to understand better the mechanisms of the business cycle.
5. To conduct a computer simulation of the model described above. Computer simulation is a powerful method both for examining the logical consistency of a theoretical model and exploring its conclusions.

Chapter Summaries

Chapter 1

What are the essential features of a capitalist economy which differ from other economic systems? How do business cycles emerge from the underlying characteristics of a capitalist economy? Why are crises necessary for a capitalist economy? How does the business cycle function in assisting the reproduction, maintenance and persistence of a capitalist economy? How does the business cycle function for the stabilization of a capitalist economy? These questions are answered on the basis of Marx's *Capital.*

Chapter 2

The history of postwar Japanese business cycles is reviewed, focusing on the causes of crisis and recovery. In addition, some long-run economic data from other leading capitalist countries are shown. From these data one can see how economic variables behave in the course of business cycles. Comparing these data with the results derived from the model (*cf.* Chapter 3 and 4) we realize the fact and theory deeply. We can know what factors have been introduced into the model.

Chapter 3

In this chapter various business cycle theories are examined. However they are not depicted in the initial forms in which they were presented by their originators, instead we have constructed a series of simple models which summarizes the core of each theory and examines its dynamic properties. The results are derived by computer simulation. The theories surveyed are Marxian crisis theory and the theories of Schumpeter, Hayek and the Post-Keynesians (Samuelson, Hicks, Kaldor, Kalecki and Harrod).

Chapter 4

The fundamental model of this book is presented. The essential points are as follows: In a capitalistic economy a cumulative process of disequilibrium is generated since the disequilibrium cannot be eliminated by the so-called "price mechanism". This cumulative process must be reversed for a capitalist economy to survive. In this way business cycles are generated. It is not correct to single out a particular moment which reverses the cumulative process of disequilibrium. In this chapter the main reversing moments are explained in detail.

It is indispensable to disaggregate the economy for the analysis of the business cycle, however, it is very difficult to do so at the beginning of the analysis. So at the first stage of discussion we abstract away from the disaggregated economy, and later we construct a two-sector economic model.

Chapter 5

As a capitalist economy develops, the power of monopolistic capital and the intervention of the government increase. How the performance of the business cycle is changed by these factors is examined in Chapter 5. The central problem is whether the intervention of government succeeds in alleviating the cumulative growth of disequilibrium or not. In spite of the economic intervention by government (Keynesianism), capitalism cannot escape from its contradictions. It is shown what democratic reforms and/or policies are necessary.

Authors

Nobuo Okishio (Chapter 1)
Faculty of Economics, Osaka Keizai University
Emeritus Professor of Faculty of Economics, Kobe University

Masato Sato (Chapter 2)
Faculty of Economics, Kansai University

Yoshikazu Sato (Chapter 3 section 1, section 2 [3] [4] [5] [6])
Faculty of Economics, Toyama University

The late Yoichi Aiba (Chapter 3 section 2 [1] [2])

Taiji Hagiwara (Chapter 4 section 1, 2 ,4)
Faculty of Economics, Kobe University

Yasutaka Niisato (Chapter 4 section 3, 4)
Faculty of Economics, Toyama University

Takeshi Nakatani (Chapter 5)
Faculty of Economics, Kobe University

Yasuki Ochi (Programs)
Faculty of Humanity, Kochi University

Acknowledgement

We are grateful to Prof. Michael Krüger who gave us a chance to publish our book one of the series Dynamische Wirtschaftstheorie. Mr. Robert McCormick made tremendous effort to make the English more readable and understandable.

In addition, we appreciate to Ms. Iris Kramer-Alcorn (Peter Lang Verlag) and Mr. Kaoru Sakurai (Aoki Shoten, Tokyo) for their help in editing this English version.

We have been fortunate in the assistance we have received in preparing the final manuscript. We wish to thank Ms. Yasuko Kojima, Ms. Yoshie Yamagami, Ms. Matsumi Oda and Ms. Rieko Sugasawa for their editorial corrections.

The final manuscript was typeset in MicroTEX.

Nobuo Okishio
Yoshikazu Sato
Managing Editor of the English version

Contents

Chapter 1

Capitalist Society and Crisis

1.1 Problems on the Crisis Theory

In my opinion, there are three problems to be solved concerning crisis theory:

1. Crises and business cycles are characteristic phenomena in capitalist society.
2. Crises and business cycles are indispensable for the reproduction of capitalist society.
3. Crises and business cycles create the conditions to abolish capitalist society and bring forth new relations of production.

These three points derive from the study the political economy of capitalism whose central questions reveal the following three themes:

1. Capitalism is a unique social form which appeared at a particular stage in human history.
2. Capitalism contains a self-reproductive mechanism in itself.
3. Capitalism creates the conditions to abolish itself and produce a new social form.

By making these themes clear political economy can grasp capitalism both historically and totally. To grasp capitalism historically it is not sufficient to simply show that capitalism is a particular historical form of human society; it is also necessary to demonstrate that the self-reproduction of capitalism creates new conditions which are incompatible with its existence and thereby abolishes itself. On the other hand, to comprehend capitalism totally it is necessary to elucidate the very foundations of the system, making clear the mechanisms by which capitalism maintains and reproduces itself, and show how capitalism creates the conditions to abolish itself.[1] Illustrating the above three problems, we get the following figure:

Figure 1.1

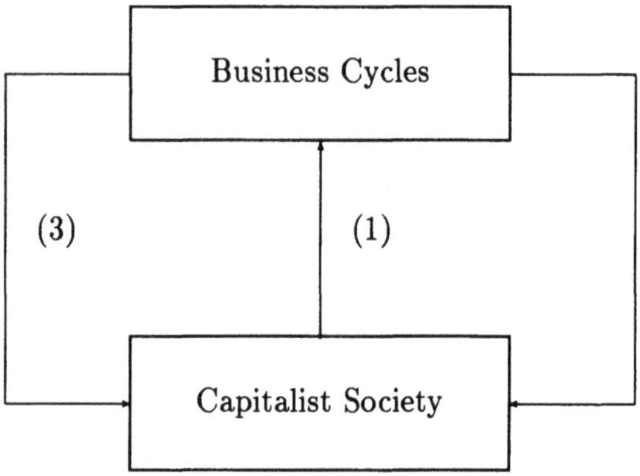

There has been a great amount of crisis theory literature. Though none of it has addressed the above three problems explicitly, I believe there are few Marxian economists who would deny their validity. Marx stated that his economic methodology was dialectical. The dialectic "includes in its comprehension an affirmative recognition of the existing state of things, at the same time also, the recognition of the negation of that state, of its inevitable breaking up; because it regards every historically developed social form as in fluid movement, its momentary existence".[2]

[1]The third problem is the most important task of economics. On this point my opinion is different from the so called "Uno-theory". Concerning about "Uno-theory", see, e.g. Makoto Itoh, *Value and Crisis - Essays on Marxian Economics in Japan -*, Monthly Press, 1980.

[2]K.Marx, *Capital* volume I, in the afterward of the second edition.

So far, a tremendous emphasis has been laid on the first problem, and the second and third have not received proper treatment.

Though it is natural, as it is the basis of crisis theory, to emphasize the first problem, the second and third, especially the latter, must be explored more deeply if we wish to grasp capitalism historically and totally.

1.2 Characteristics of Capitalism

One of the main distinguishing characteristics of capitalism is that it is a class society. Here class society means a society where the decisions about production, (what, how much, how, when and how to dispose of) are monopolized by a few members of society and others are excluded from this decision making process. People excluded from the decision making are compelled to work subject to the decisions made by the privileged few and are exploited for their surplus labour. The decisions about production are formulated by the privileged in order to exploit the majority. Workers receive only a portion of the net output, *i.e.* the residual of output after deducting the replacement of production goods required to reproduce the society at the same scale in the next period. The exploiting class obtains the rest (surplus output) and spends it on their own consumption, "non-reproductive exhaustion" to maintain the class society, additional investment to increase production in the next period, and other sorts of waste.

Another main characteristic by which capitalism is distinguished from other social forms is the prevalence of commodity production. In spite of the fact that a social division of labour prevails under capitalism, the means of production in every sector of that division of labour are privately owned; hence decisions on production are both private and dispersed and the output of production is owned privately. Therefore the products are fated to be commodities produced for exchange purposes, and social and material reproduction is obliged to be carried out through the exchange of commodities. However the overall exchange of commodities is carried out only by indirect exchange through the medium of money as illustrated here.[3]

[3]The owner of commodity A can get B in direct exchange for commodity A, only when the owner of commodity B wants to exchange commodity B for commodity A. But the owner of commodity B may possibly want commodity C. In this case the owner of commodity A may be forced to examine the possibility of getting commodity B in indirect exchange.

Commodity A – Money – Commodity B

Consequently each exchange is decomposed into the simple exchange (purchase and sale): Commodity – Money. Commodities cannot be obtained without money. Workers, who are alienated from the private ownership of means of production and own nothing but labour power, must transform their labour power into money, that is, sell it, and therefore they become wage workers. Thus not only all products but also labour power become commodities and are valued in terms of money and priced. Thereafter the private and dispersed decisions of capitalists are made on the basis of the rate of the profit which is the ratio between the money advanced and the profit realized (proceeds minus costs).

The first problem, identified above, is to derive the inevitability of crisis and business cycle from these two characteristics of capitalism.

1.3 The Anarchy of Production and Disequilibrium

A social division of labour prevails in capitalism. Various types of means of production are necessary to produce a commodity, but these means of production themselves must be produced as commodities in other sectors. Moreover in order to reproduce labour power, daily necessities must be produced in other sectors. These means of production and daily necessities must not only be produced, but also be properly distributed in order to make possible reproduction in the next period.

Under capitalism there does not exist a central decision making process concerning all social production. Each process within the division of labour

That is to say, if all goes well, he first exchanges commodity A for commodity C, and then obtains commodity B in exchange for commodity C. But if the owner of commodity C wants something else, another indirect exchange is required, the series of indirect exchanges soon becomes so long that a lot of information and time is necessary for these exchanges. Therefore such exchanges become an obstacle to the smooth reproduction of society. But these difficulties can be solved with the simplest method of unified indirect exchange, where all owners exchange their commodities for money. This makes it possible for any commodity to be exchanged for any other.

is left to the private and dispersed decisions of capitalists. Capitalists are obliged to direct production on the basis of profit rates which are predicted on the basis of the limited local information available to them.[4] It would be almost miraculous in such a situation if production coincided with social equilibrium. Disequilibrium invariably occurs. Produced commodities may not be demanded at the price predicted at the time of the production decision, and conversely may not fulfill demand. Excess demand or excess supply will occur. Labour expended on the basis of private decision (private labour) cannot obtain social recognition on the prior predicted condition, but obtains recognition in the market on better or worse conditions.

But this disequilibrium does not immediately cause a crisis and business cycle because capitalism has a mechanism which ameliorates it. The prices of commodities in excess demand rise, and those in excess supply fall. This may induce capitalists to alter their production decisions and thus may clear the market by increasing production in the former case or decreasing production in the latter. Even in a situation where prices are inflexible due to the tightness of markets, information about unfilled demand in the case of excess demand, or goods left unsold in the case of excess supply, may induce capitalists to increase production in the former case or decrease production in the latter. If a mechanism of this sort always works smoothly, the disequilibrium which is caused by the anarchy of production in capitalism will always be dissolved without a crisis and business cycle.

Therefore, in order to assert that crises and business cycles are inevitable in capitalism, we must show why the disequilibrium which is caused by the anarchy of capitalist production cannot be smoothly adjusted to an equilibrium condition, but must cumulative unilaterally in spite of the existence of the mechanism mentioned above.

1.4 The Conditions of Equilibrium

Capitalism is a class society where the production of commodities prevails. The aggregated product must be sold as commodities. A portion of the ag-

[4]Since the 1970s, an economic theory based on "Rational Expectations" has prevailed. In such economics all participants in capitalism are assumed to behave with perfect expectations of the future economic situation. This theory ignores one of the characteristics of capitalism.

gregated product is bought by capitalists for the replacement of production goods. Part of the rest (the net product) is bought with the wages of workers. But that is only a part of the net product because workers are exploited and therefore unable to purchase the total net product. The residual, which remains after deducting workers' consumption from net output, is the surplus product. The consumption demand of capitalists is not sufficient to absorb these commodities. This is because capitalists, who are the exploiting class in capitalism, differ from the exploiting classes of previous class societies in that they exploit workers not only for their own consumption but also for accumulation of surplus value expressed as money. Therefore the consumption of capitalists accounts for only a part of the total profit and consequently the surplus product cannot be exhausted by the consumption of capitalists alone. In order for the surplus product to be realized, an additional demand of capitalists or accumulation demand (a demand for the expansion of production in the next period) is indispensable.[5]

The problem here is to show how disequilibrium becomes cumulative in cap italism. To achieve this, we shall consider how the capitalist economy must move in every period to maintain equilibrium. Marx answered this problem with his famous scheme of extended production. We present it here in a simpler form:[6]

$$X = C + V + M_k + I \tag{1.1}$$

$$M_k = k(X - C - V) \tag{1.2}$$

$$C = aX \tag{1.3}$$

[5]We neglect the demand of government and foreign countries.

[6]Though Marx gave, as is well known, a reproduction scheme of two sectors, we use here the aggregate scheme for simplicity. Note that though the equation $C = aX$ means the technical relation, the equation $V = bX$, means not only the technical relation, but also exploitation. Denoting living labour and surplus value by N and M respectively, we have $N = V + M$. And from

$$V = \frac{N}{X}\frac{V}{N}X$$

we have

$$b = \frac{N}{X}\frac{1}{1 + M/V}$$

so b depends upon technical relation N/X and the rate of exploitation M/V.

$$V = bX \tag{1.4}$$

$$I = (a + b)\Delta X \tag{1.5}$$

The left side of equation (1.1) denotes the value of the aggregate product and the right-hand side denotes demand. C is the replacement demand, V is the consumption demand of workers, M_k is the consumption demand of capitalists, and I is the accumulation demand. Therefore equation (1.1) indicates that aggregate supply equals aggregate demand. Equation (1.2) indicates that consumption of capitalists is a fixed portion of profit. Equations (1.3) and (1.4) indicate the normal relations among constant capital, variable capital and aggregate product value. The fifth equation shows that the additional capital procured by the demand for accumulation in this period works normally in the next period. ΔX denotes the difference between the aggregate product of the next period and that of this period. In order that the commodities supplied are equal to aggregate demand, and for capital to work normally in every period, the above five equations must hold. Following from equations (1.1) through (1.5) we have:

$$\frac{\Delta X}{X} = \frac{I}{(a+b)X} = \frac{(1-k)(1-a-b)}{a+b} \tag{1.6}$$

The rate of profit r is given by:

$$r = \frac{X - C - V}{C + V} \tag{1.7}$$

So, (1.6) can be rewritten as:

$$\frac{\Delta X}{X} = \frac{I}{(a+b)X} = r(1-k) = g* \tag{1.8}$$

In order that supply equals demand and that capital works normally in every period, the growth rate of production and capital must be $r(1-k)$, where r is profit rate and $(1-k)$ is the saving rate of capitalists. We shall write $r(1-k)$ as g^* hereafter.

1.5 Cumulative Disequilibrium

Now let us suppose that the growth rate of capital (the rate of capital accumulation) is larger (smaller) than equilibrium rate $g*$ given by (1.6) or (1.7). What situation will come about?

If the growth rate of capital is greater than g^*, then by (1.6):

$$I > (1-k)(1-a-b) \tag{1.9}$$

Which can be rewritten by (1.2) through (1.4) as:

$$I > X - C - V - M_k \tag{1.10}$$

This means:

$$X < C + V + M_k + I \tag{1.11}$$

which shows that an excess demand has occurred. If instead the growth rate of capital is less than $g*$ there will be an excess supply in the commodity market.

Thus, the state of the economy definitely depends upon the growth rate of capital. What determines the capitalists' demand for accumulation I? Not a few people still insist on the false idea that accumulation demand is identically equal to the residual surplus value after capitalists' consumption.

$$I = M - M_k = (1-k)(X - C - V) \tag{1.12}$$

If this is true, $M = M_k + I$. Considering $M = X - C - V$, the equality $X = C + V + M_k + I$ holds identically. This means that aggregate demand for commodities is always equal to aggregate supply (Say's "market law"). Therefore, it be impossible for general over-production to occur.

These people have the false idea that residual surplus value after capitalist consumption is always directed to additional demand for commodities as a demand for accumulation. However those residuals are not always spent for commodities, some of them may take the form of an increase in money or financial assets held by capitalists. Being financed by credit, accumulation demand for commodities may exceed those residuals $(M - M_k)$.

Another cause of their error is their belief that the demand for accumulation in this period is financed by the surplus value which is realized in the same period. As shown above, capitalists' consumption and accumulation is necessary in order to realize the surplus product in this period. Therefore the realized surplus value in this period depends on the demand for accumulation. So it is incorrect to contend that the demand for accumulation in the current period depends on realized surplus value in the same.

Capitalists determine their demand for accumulation based on the expectation of realizing future surplus value subject to various considerations: existing capital stock, market situations, finance conditions *etc.*. The most important factor in the formation of expectations is the contemporary economic situation. They form expectations by interpreting this situation. Factors involved in expectation formation are the tightness of markets, prices, wage rates, profit rates and so on. As mentioned above, if the growth rate of capital is larger (smaller) than the equilibrium rate g^*, excess demand (excess supply) occurs in the commodity markets. When commodity markets are in excess demand (excess supply), prices are higher (lower) relative to the wage rate and the profit rate is also higher (lower). Capitalists will increase (decrease) the growth rate of capital further responding to the excess demand (excess supply) in the commodity market.[7]

Accordingly the degree of excess demand (excess supply) is accelerated. In this way, disequilibrium in the commodity market accumulates.

1.6 The Necessity of Crises and Business Cycles

In capitalism, owing to the predominance of commodity production, social reproduction depends wholly on the realization of commodities in markets. Moreover, because of the existence of exploitation, accumulation demand plays a decisive role in the realization of commodities. And since this accumulation demand is determined by individual capitalists in a private and

[7]It is the condition of cumulative disequilibrium that capitalists increase (decrease) the growth rate of capital in response to excess demand (supply). The mere increase (decrease) of the level of accumulation demand does not always create a cumulative disequilibrium.

unintegrated fashion, the capitalist economy tends to accumulate disequilibrium despite the existence of a price adjustment mechanism.[8]

If such a cumulative process of disequilibrium is left unimproved, capitalism eventually becomes unable to reproduce itself. The upward cumulative process in which excess demand is accelerating may seem to be happy for everybody. Capitalists experience a high rate of profit, excess demand for their commodities, and an abnormally high rate of utilization of their capital.

At the same time, workers are experiencing increasing employment and are earning growing real wages. Indeed it is seemingly a time of great "prosperity".[9] But ultimately the upward cumulative process of disequilibrium makes the reproduction of capitalism impossible, because the means of production sector grows faster than the consumption goods sector, and the real wage rate (the quantity of consumption goods purchasable with the money wage per unit of labour) begins to fall. Eventually the absolute quantity of consumption goods which workers can purchase decreases.[10] Consequently the reproduction of labour power becomes impossible. And then the reproduction of capitalism is also impossible.

In the downward cumulative process of disequilibrium in which excess supply accelerates, unemployment increases and the realized rate of profit falls. When the capitalist class loses the ability to employ wage labour, capitalism becomes fragile. The capitalist class is able to rule the working class because wage workers cannot live without selling their labour and

[8]In capitalism, crises inevitably come about because of the tendency for the system to accumulate disequilibrium. And the disequilibrium is accumulated, not only because there exists "the production of commodities ", but also because of the existence of exploitation and the special way in which decisions about accumulation demand are made. It is important to understand this, when we consider the role which the production of commodities plays in socialism.

[9]In a boom, consumption is always depressed relative to the additional production goods for accumulation. Therefore the boom is a "hard" period in which people are forced the sacrifice for accumulation. But in capitalism the boom appears as a prosperous time for capitalists, and even for workers because unemployment decreases despite a rise in the rate of exploitation.

[10]This is easily understood from the following extreme case. In full employment the upward cumulative process is carried out through the shift of workers from the consumption goods sector to the means of production goods sector. So the output of consumption goods decreases, therefore the consumption goods earned by the working class would decrease even if they could receive all of the consumption goods produced.

capitalists can buy that labour and pay workers the wages which are their means of livelihood.

Therefore, capitalism must reverse the cumulative process of disequilibrium in order to reproduce itself. It must convert the upward cumulative process into a downward cumulative process. And likewise it must turn a downward process into an upward process. Thus capitalism is obliged to have business cycles. The necessity of crises and business cycles are found here.

1.7 Reversing the Upward Cumulative Process of Disequilibrium

The moment in which to reverse the upward cumulative process of disequilibrium cannot be predetermined a priori. Most authors on crisis theory have discussed various moments when an upward cumulative process is reversed, and have regarded these studies as a proof of the necessity of economic crises. In my opinion, however, a proof of the necessity of economic crises is completely given by showing, as discussed above, that a cumulative process of disequilibrium inevitably arises, and the reproduction of capitalistic society becomes impossible unless such a process is reversed.

It is not correct to pick only one specific moment which reverses the cumulative process and then generalize that the cumulative process is necessarily reversed by this moment. We cannot deduce a unique moment of reversal merely from the fundamental characteristics of capitalist society. More detailed and concrete studies are needed to identify the moment. That man must necessarily die can be proved from the characteristics of the human body. However the moment of death is not necessarily pre-determined. In which moment it takes place, and whether by cancer, suicide, nuclear bomb or other means, depends on concrete conditions. Some possible and probable moments for the reversal of an upward cumulative process of disequilibrium are considered here.

1.7.1 A Fall in the Rate of Profit in the Consumption Goods Sector

At the beginning of an upward cumulative disequilibrium process demand exceeds supply and the rate of profit rises in both the means of production sector and the consumption goods sector. However while this process is going on, other circumstances may arise: Accumulation demand, during the upward cumulative process, is mainly for means of production and therefore the prices in that sector rise faster than the prices of consumption goods. As a result the rate of profit in the consumption goods sector may fall, even if the price of consumption goods rises relative to the money wage rate and if the rate of exploitation rises.[11] Capitalists in the consumption goods sector decrease their accumulation demand corresponding to the fall in their profit rate, and if capitalists in means of production sector follow it, then the upward cumulative disequilibrium process may be reversed.

1.7.2 Bottleneck in the Production Goods Sector

In an upward cumulative process demand for means of production rapidly increases as a result of an accelerated accumulation demand. The amount of means of production which can be used for the purpose of accumulation is, however, restricted by the surplus means of production which remain after deducting replacement demand in both sectors. Production takes time. Therefore the surplus means of production are fixed at any given point in time. If demand exceeds this amount additional surplus means of production can be produced subject to a time lag. But for the time being there arises a bottleneck of means of production and the planned accumulation demand cannot be totally satisfied. This may result in a downward revision of accumulation plans and a corresponding retardation of investment demand. Thus the upward cumulative disequilibrium process may be reversed.

[11] In this case, the capitalists in the consumption goods sector exploit workers further, then their production of surplus value increases. However they are squeezed by the capitalists in the means of production sector through a rise in its prices, so their surplus value obtained may decreases.

1.7.3 Restriction of the Labour Force

The unemployment rate falls and the money wage rate rises in an upward cumulative process. Its effect on the rate of profit depends upon the movement of commodity prices. If commodity prices rise more rapidly than the money wage rate, the real wage rate falls and the rate of profit rises. The movement of commodity prices depends upon supply and demand conditions in the commodity markets. When capitalists accelerate their accumulation demand, commodity prices rise more rapidly relative to the money wage rate. But after the unemployed are totally absorbed, it becomes impossible to increase employment as a whole (although it may be possible, to some extent, by extending the length of the working day). In order for capitalists in some sector A to increase the labour force available to them, they must take away workers employed in the other sector B. In order to succeed, capitalists in sector A must increase the money wage rate enough to make the real wage rate in terms of the prices of products from sector B greater than the labour productivity in B. In sector B the capitalists are obliged to part with their workers as a result of the rising real wages, there then develops idle capacity of equipment and a fall of the rate of profit and thus a decline in the accumulation demand. In sector A, where the capitalists have succeeded in acquiring additional workers, the rate of profit does not necessarily fall and the accumulation demand will continue to increase.[12] Nevertheless, the upward cumulative process may be halted as a result of the declining accumulation demand in the sector from which workers were removed. And this may cause a crisis.

1.7.4 Credit Restriction

An upward cumulative process is caused by an accelerated increase in accumulation demand by capitalists. This acceleration, as has already been stated, requires an acceleration in credit. If the accumulation demand is

[12]The rate of profit in some sectors depends upon the real wage rate measured by that sector's product. In the sector deprived of workers (the consumption goods sector) the money wage rate rises relative to the prices of consumption goods, then the rate of profit declines. Conversely, in the sector acquiring workers (the means of production sector) the price rises relative to the money wage rate, therefore the real wage rate measured by means of production goods may decline.

financed by the remainder of profits which are not spent on consumption, additional credit is not necessary. However, if this is the case, even an equilibrium rate of growth cannot be guaranteed[13], and a downward, not upward, cumulative process ensues. Credit expansion is generated by both firms and banks. There is a close, mutual relationship between credit expansion and the supply and demand conditions in commodity markets. Credit expansion guarantees an acceleration in the increase in accumulation demand and a continuance of excess demand in commodity markets. Moreover, a continuance of excess demand in commodity markets creates optimistic expectations and brings about further credit expansion. Therefore both factors are simultaneously causes and effects of each other in the upward cumulative process. If credit extension is slowed down for any reason, the interest rate rises and the acceleration of accumulation demand may come to a standstill.

1.8 Reversing the Downward Cumulative Process of Disequilibrium

Moments to reverse a downward cumulative process of disequilibrium are also not predetermined. Some possible and probable moments are listed below.

1.8.1 A Rise in the Profit Rate in the Consumption Goods Sector

We have already discussed the possibility of an upward cumulative process being reversed by a fall in the rate of profit in the consumption goods sec-

[13]Capitalists certainly decide the level of their consumption and accumulation demands in expectation of the profits realized in this period. But such demands cannot be financed by the profits realized in this period. Because the profits of this period are realized by the demands of capitalists' consumption and accumulation of this period. If the demands are financed by the profits realized in the last period, the profits realized in this period is no more than that in the last period. And as the production capacity of this period is larger than that of the last period, due to accumulation, there is, necessarily, excess supply or under utilization of capital equipment.

tor. There the prices of means of production goods rose faster than that of consumption goods which rose faster than the money wage rate, and this resulted in a fall in the rate of profit in the consumption goods sector. The exact converse may occur in a downward process. Namely an accelerating contraction in accumulation demand results in excess supply and prices fall in the commodity markets. And the prices of means of production goods fall faster than the price of consumption goods which, in turn, fall faster than the money wage rate. Therefore in the consumption goods sector there may occur an increase in the rate of profit as a result of the relative decrease in the prices of means of production goods relative to the prices of consumption goods, notwithstanding a rise in the real wage rate in terms of consumption goods. Thus the accumulation demand of the consumption goods sector may expand, and this may lead to an increase in the overall accumulation demand, which converts the downward process into an upward one.

1.8.2 Enforced Introduction of New Technologies

In a downward cumulative process unemployment increases and the money wage rate decreases. However, the real wage rate increases as a result of the much greater decrease in commodity prices caused by the accelerated contraction in accumulation demand. An increase in the real wage rate brings about a fall in the rate of exploitation, which eventually diminishes to zero if production technologies remain unchanged. At this point capitalists are compelled to choose either bankruptcy or the introduction of new technologies. The introduction of new technologies requires a certain necessary minimum fund and capitalists who do not possess it are obliged to drop out. Those who can afford to introduce new technologies are able to prevent the rate of exploitation from declining and may even succeed in raising it by increasing labour productivity. An accumulation demand created by the introduction of new technologies results in a recovery and even an increase in the aggregate demand which may reverse the downward cumulative process.

1.8.3 Capitalists' Consumption Demand

In a downward cumulative process replacement demand, workers' consumption, and accumulation demand all contract. Capitalists' consumption demands also decrease according to the fall in realized profit. Capitalists' consumption, however, differs in character from workers' consumption in the sense that capitalists' consumption is not restricted by their actually realized profit income. Their consumption demand does not decrease beyond some minimum level no matter how severely their realized profits are cut. To this minimum amount of capitalists' consumption there corresponds a certain level of production. When the capitalist economy collapses to this extremely low level, there is no replacement demand for durable equipment and production continues with existing equipment. However, with the passage of time, existing equipment depreciates and eventually cannot maintain the required level of production which corresponds to the consumption of the capitalist class. This causes a rise in the demand for means of production which may result in a recovery and an increase of the accumulation demand.

1.9 Fundamental Contradiction in Capitalism and Crisis

Capitalism is a class society in which commodity production prevails. With commodity production the problem of realization occurs and disequilibrium inevitably results. This is because decisions about production are made privately by individuals in spite of the social division of labour. This economic anarchy is a necessary condition for crises and business cycles.[14] However, it is not a sufficient condition. Difficulties of realization and disequilibrium do not necessarily induce a crisis and business cycle. Even if disequilibrium occurs, it can be equilibrated by the price mechanism without crisis, unless the disequilibrium is cumulative in one direction.

The cumulative nature of disequilibrium arises from the fact that capitalism is not only a commodity producing society but also a class society. Decisions on production are taken by private capitalists, who make deci-

[14]K.Marx discussed "the abstract possibility of crisis" in volume I of *Kapital.*

sions in the interests of profitability with only local and short-sighted information. Correspondingly, workers are excluded from decision-making and obliged to become wage workers condemned to exploitation. When workers are exploited, capitalists' accumulation demand becomes indispensable for the realization of the value of commodities, and thus it becomes an important determinant of aggregate demand. Because decisions on accumulation demand are made by private capitalists, accumulation demand moves the economy towards a condition of cumulative disequilibrium. And this cumulative process must be necessarily reversed by a crisis and business cycle for capitalism to be reproduced. Thus crisis is inevitable in capitalism.

Usually the "fundamental contradiction of capitalism" is formulated as the contradiction between the social characteristics of production and private capitalist appropriation. This formulation is thought to summarize the two basic characteristics of capitalism: commodity production and class society. Therefore we can say that crisis and business cycle are an inevitable result of the fundamental contradiction of capitalism.

Most Marxian economists regard "the contradiction between production and consumption" as the most important factor in explaining crises.[15] It is said that in spite of the fact that capitalists accelerate production in the search for profit, workers' consumption is depressed due to exploitation, and capitalists' consumption is limited by accumulation, so inevitably there arises the difficulty of realizing commodity values. This reasoning is erroneous. Even if production is increased, and the consumption demands of workers and capitalists are limited, a difficulty in realization does not necessarily occur. Because, as shown above, an acceleration of production can be absorbed by a further increase in the demand for accumulation.

We consider "the contradiction between production and consumption" as a dispensable factor in explaining crises for a different reason than the one above. First let us interpret "the contradiction" as the existence of a gap between production and consumption. Which of the following does "production" mean?
(a) The production of consumption goods

[15]"The ultimate reason for all real crises always remains the poverty and restricted consumption of the masses as opposed to the drive of capitalist production to develop productive forces as though only the absolute consuming power of society constituted their limit." K.Marx, *Capital* in volume III part IV chapter 30.

(b) the aggregate product including consumption goods and means of production goods, or
(c) the net product which is the balance of the aggregate product after deducting the replacement of the used up means of production.

If (a), "the contradiction" signifies a discrepancy between the production of consumption goods and consumption demand. But excess supply in the consumption goods sector cannot always be observed and crises does not necessarily begin in that sector. If (b), it means a difference between consumption goods plus production goods and consumption demand. But this inequality must hold in every society, because for social reproduction it is necessary to produce the means of production to replace depleted means of production. So it is not a contradiction.

Therefore "production" must be taken to mean (c) the net product. Net product workers' consumption + capitalists' consumption implies net products workers' consumption. Assuming workers' consumption = wages, it means net product is greater than wage,*i.e.*, exploitation. Thus it becomes clear that the contradiction between production and consumption thus interpreted is nothing but the existence of exploitation. As repeatedly stated exploitation is a basic factor in causing crisis. Owing to exploitation, capital accumulation demand becomes indispensable to realize commodity values and this is one of the main causes of cumulative disequilibrium.

If we interpret "the contradiction between production and consumption" not as the existence of a gap between production and consumption but as a gap between the rates of growth of production and consumption, how can we show the relationship between "the contradiction" and crisis? Here "production" means the net product. Therefore the "contradiction" is here understood to mean an increase in the gap between the net product and consumption. For this gap to continue to increase, capitalists must accelerate the increase accumulation demand. In the upward cumulative process of disequilibrium we observe this very fact. However, as demonstrated above in section seven, the thus interpreted "contradiction" can not last forever, because it renders capitalism unable to reproduce itself. Therefore its reversing by crisis becomes inevitable.

1.10 Capitalist Reproduction and Crisis

Capitalism, by its very nature, produces a cumulative process of disequilibrium. And unless this process is reversed in due time, capitalism cannot reproduce itself. This reversing is carried out by a crisis and business cycle. In this sense crisis plays a necessary and indispensable role for capitalist reproduction. Let us consider this point from several perspectives.

1.10.1 Equilibrating "the Gap Between Production and Consumption"

Owing to exploitation, capitalism always generates a gap between the net product and consumption. This gap grows wider during the upward cumulative process. Unlimited widening of this gap would render capitalism unable to reproduce itself. It is a crisis that reverses the upward process into a downward one. In this reversal the gap between net product and consumption begins to shrink. In other words, an equilibrating process of contradiction between production and consumption starts.

However, this equilibrating process is also full of contradictions. In the upward cumulative process, though consumption is depressed, an increasing part of the net product is absorbed in the accumulation demand. Accumulation accelerates the increase of productive capacity. When accumulation demand contracts, aggregate demand shrinks and the consumption demands of workers also decrease. Consequently, the productive capacity which has been amassed by depressing the consumption of the working class, *i.e.* by strengthening exploitation, cannot be utilized normally and excess supply appears in the commodity market. In response, capitalists decrease accumulation demand further, and aggregate demand and production shrink still more. It is true that the gap between net product and consumption shrinks in this process, however, it is done not by increasing consumption, but by decreasing production which is accompanied by severe unemployment and idle capacity.[16]

[16]The gap between production and consumption is not smoothly adjusted in capitalism. We can easily understand the peculiar character of the adjustment process if we make a comparison between such processes in socialism and capitalism. The period of accelerated accumulation, as stated in footnote 10, is a hard time for socialism. And when people

1.10.2 Equalizing Profit Rates

In the upward cumulative process, owing to the acceleration of accumulation demand, the degree of excess demand and the over utilization of productive capacity is much severer in the producer goods sector than in the consumption goods sector. Therefore the rate of profit in the means of production sector rises more rapidly than in the consumption goods sector. Due to the movements of profit rates, the share of the means of production sector increases relative to the consumption goods sector (the so-called preferential progress of the means of production sector). When accumulation demand begins to shrink, this movement is reversed. The prices of producer goods begin to decrease faster than the prices of consumption goods and the money wage rate. The rate of profit in the producer goods sector declines more rapidly than in the consumption goods sector. And the weight of the consumption goods sector increases relatively to the means of production sector. Through such reversals the difference in profit rates of the two sectors is prevented from accumulating and rates of profit are approximately equalized.[17]

1.10.3 The Reproduction of Wage Labour

The most important circumstance for capitalism to reproduce is the persistent regular and repeated appearance of workers in the labour market

require no more accumulation, they decide to utilize the production capacity that has been accumulated for their own consumption. When the gap between production and consumption disappears, they will have a happy time. On the contrary, under capitalism the cessation of accumulation causes a crisis, a downward cumulative process, resulting in unemployment and hard times.

[17]One of the propositions which constitutes "the labour theory of value", is that prices of commodities are mainly determined by their value (social standard bestowed labour). This proposition is deduced from the tendency that equalizes the rate of profits in each sector (the theory of production price). However, the equal rate of profit is not realized through a smooth adjustment process: high(low) rate of profit entrance(withdrawal) of capitals excess-supply (-demand) decline (rise) of price decline (rise) in the rate of profit. Instead, it is realized through a crisis and business cycle. On this point our theory is different from neoclassical price adjustment theory (or "Uno Theory").

to sell their labour power. This is guaranteed by confining the real wage and employment within a certain range.[18] As to real wage, it must not be less than a minimum level which is determined both physically and socially. On the other hand, it must not be large enough for workers to afford the purchase of the means of production. Also it must not be so large that capitalists are unable to exploit workers. In terms of employment, unemployment must remain above a certain level. Otherwise, capitalists can not maintain control over workers with the threat of dismissal. On the other hand, the rate of unemployment must be too high, or workers will no longer expect to be employed and capitalists will lose their hegemony.

Crisis and business cycle is the mechanism by which the real wage and employment are confined within a suitable range. In the upward cumulative process a decrease in unemployment and a decline in the real wage rate compared with labour productivity occurs. In the downward cumulative process an increase in unemployment and a rise in the real wage rate relative to labour productivity occurs. The switching from one process to the other preserves the real wage and employment within the appropriate range for capitalist reproduction.

1.11 Transcendence of the Capitalist System and Crisis

Crises and business cycles are necessary to the reproduction of the capitalist system. In this sense crises and business cycles work as the reproductive mechanism of the capitalist system. However, in contrast, we must consider whether or not this movement, which is indispensable for the reproduction of the system, creates factors that necessitate replacing the capitalist system with other new relations of production. That is the question.

[18] "The value of labour power", which plays an important part in Kapital by K.Marx, means the value of the consumption goods necessary to reproduce labour power. Here the reproduction of the labour force must be the reproduction of "wage labour power". In order to reproduce it, it is not necessary for real wage rate to keep a certain level but to be confined within a certain range, where wage workers are compelled to reappear at labour market even if the money wage rates rise or decline.

1.11.1 Incompatible Productive power

The capitalist system could not reproduce itself if the downward cumulative process were not reversed, and it is the revival or increase of accumulation demand due to the introduction of new technologies that is most important in the turnaround moments. In the capitalist system new techniques are introduced and production equipment embodying old ones are scrapped in the course of a business cycle. In this way, productive power increases in the capitalist system.

The increase of productive power brought about by the introduction of new techniques plays an important part in the reproduction and survival of the capitalist system. By raising labour productivity through an introduction of new techniques, capitalists can prevent the profit rate from declining even if they concede to increased real wages for workers. And by increasing labour productivity and the technical composition of capital it becomes possible, in the long run, for the capital accumulation rate and the growth rate of products to rise over the imitations of the increasing rate of labour supply in the capitalist system.

But capitalistic relations of production are not compatible with any level of productive power. In general, for any given system, it is necessary that productive power be kept within a definite range in order for the specific relations of production to continue to function. If productive power exceeds some upper limit, it becomes difficult for the specific relations of production to reproduce themselves within that system. Capitalism is no exception.

It is inevitable, with the constant expansion in productive power, that eventually that same power will become incompatible with the capitalist system. We consider four possible forms such incompatibility might take:
(a) With increasing labour productivity the problem of unemployment and realization becomes acute, propelling the capitalist system into instability.
(b) The enormous funds necessary to develop or introduce new technologies may outstrip the abilities of private capitalists to assemble. This leads to the introduction of public funding by the national state, which contradicts the principle of private capital investment, and thus bribery and corruption prevail.
(c) New technologies bring about widespread and dangerous changes into the life environment of human beings, the human body and nature. Under these conditions, it imperils human beings' survival to entrust decisions on

production to anarchic private capitalists.
(d) New technologies have spectacularly increased information processing capabilities. Not only have the material conditions which support advanced data processing emerged, but the abilities of the members of society to make use of these new capabilities has also increased remarkably. It will become increasingly difficult to exclude majorities proficient in the new information technologies from taking part in production decisions, even though this exclusion is the very foundation of capitalism.[19]

1.11.2 The Formation of Revolutionary People

As the productive power of humans comes to have a character incompatible with capitalistic relations of production, human society cannot help choosing either of the following two alternatives. One, maintain capitalistic relations of production by any and all means (interventions of the state, maneuvers over the working class, suppression, and military power *etc.*). The other is to replace the relations of production with new ones, which are characterized by fundamental production decisions being made socially, not privately. The former deepens the inconsistency between the characteristics of the new productive powers and the relations of production, and, sooner or later, will endanger the survival of human beings. The latter alternative creates new relations of production which conform to the new productive powers and guarantee the survival of human beings. Therefore, we must choose the latter alternative for the future survival of human society.

Undoubtedly, this important choice has to be made by human beings themselves. How are the people who would choose the latter alternative developed? Crises and business cycles play an important role in the formation of such people. The working classes are forced to suffer unemployment in a downward cumulative process. Production capacity, which has been accumulated by raising the rate of exploitation during the upward cumulative process, remains idle. In the upward cumulative process, unemployment of workers declines but the rate of exploitation rises. The introduction of new technology compels workers to endure unemployment and disruption,

[19]See N. Okishio "Notes on Technical Progress and Capitalist Society ", *Cambridge Journal of Economics* 1977, vol.1, No.1.

as well as the devaluation of formerly valuable skills. The pressure on capitalists in the downward cumulative process forces minor capitalists, unable to raise funds for the new technology, into bankruptcy. The increase of new productive powers raises information processing capabilities which is the foundation of the capacity for decision making of ordinary people including the working class. At present, the productive powers monopolized by the capitalist class are employed in ways that bring about widespread, serious and irreversible damages and dangers to the life environment, human body and nature. All of these experiences increase the number of people who recognize that the replacement of the current relations of production is a necessity.

Of course it is one sided, if we do not consider the opposition of capitalism to the increase of such people. When the working class or minor capitalists get into trouble economically, they are apt to turn to "big men" for salvation who will exploit these opportunities. In spite of these obstacles, the majority of people either gradually or rapidly recognize the necessity of new relations of production for the survival of humanity.

Chapter 2

Statistical Evidence

2.1 Cyclical Movements

In this section we shall briefly review the statistical data on the regular changes in fundamental economic variables over the business cycle. In the next section we will examine the trends in the variables through a long series of business cycles.

2.1.1 The Growth Rate of the Economy, the Growth Rate of Investment, and the Rate of Profit

First we must define the turning points of the business cycle in order to observe how economic variables change in its various phases. Figure 2.1 shows the growth rate of real GNP, which we alternatively call the growth rate of the Japanese economy after the Second World War. The dashed lines in the figure show the turning points of the cycle as defined by the Economic Planning Agency (EPA). According to the EPA, the Japanese economy has experienced ten cycles in this period.

It is no surprise that, in general, economic growth is high and/or increases in booms and is low and/or decreases in depressions. However if one examines the figure closely, it is apparent that the turning points of business cycles, as defined by the EPA, do not always correspond to the extremities of the growth rate of the economy. This reflects a fundamental question as to how to define the phases of business cycles.

The EPA defines booms so as to include not only those periods in which the growth rate of the economy goes up, but also the short periods in which it goes down sharply after a peak. Likewise some depressions, defined by the EPA, include not only the period in which the growth rate of economy goes down, but also the short period in which it goes up after the trough. It is a matter of controversy whether the short periods after peaks in which the growth rate of economy goes down and the ones after troughs in which growth rate of economy goes up are to be regarded as booms or depressions. The answer depends on how we assign the turning points of business cycles; by the level of growth of the economy or the direction of change in it.

In order to see how changes in the fundamentals economic variables correspond to one another, we reset the turning points of business cycles according to the direction of change in the growth rate of GNP, which is the most general index of movement of an economy. Specifically, we looked for the highest growth rate of GNP in each EPA defined boom and then designated that as a "peak". Then we found the lowest growth rates between peaks and defined those points as "troughs". We characterize the periods from troughs to peaks as "upward phases", or more popularly "booms", and the periods from peaks to troughs as "downward phases" or "depressions". The turning points, according to our definition, of the post war business cycles are summarized in Table 2.1.

Table 2.1 Business Cycles in JAPAN

No.	*Trough*	*Peak*
1st cycle	1953 II	1954 I
2nd cycle	1955 I	1955 IV
3rd cycle	1958 II	1960 IV
4th cycle	1963 I	1964 I
5th cycle	1965 III	1968 IV
6th cycle	1971 III	1973 I
7th cycle	1974 I	1976 I
8th cycle	1976 IV	1977 IV
9th cycle	1982 I	1984 IV

Now that we have defined the turning points (peaks and troughs) and therefore the upward and downward phases of the business cycles, we can explore how the main variables change over the course of the business cycles. First, we shall consider investment. Figure 2.2 shows the growth rates of real GNP and real investment in Japan since the Second World War with the redefined turning points of the business cycles. It is clear that the growth rate of real investment changes in the same direction as the growth rate of real GNP but with a wider amplitude. Investment demand is widely recognized as a key component of GNP and the most volatile one. Thus we have confirmed the general idea that changes in investment demand drive changes in production in an economy as a whole.

Next we investigate the consequences of cyclical economic movements for capitalists. The rate of economic growth reveals the changes in both aggregate demand and aggregate production. Therefore it is nearly self-evident that the level of capacity utilization changes in the same direction as the growth rate of the economy.

Figure 2.3 shows how the rate of profit in the Japanese economy has varied over the course of the economic cycles of the post war period. The figure demonstrates that the rate of profit changes in the same direction as rate of economic growth in each phase of the business cycles, albeit less distinctly than investment. In particular, it is impressive that the rate of profit rose sharply during the upward phases of the 3rd quarter of 1965 to the 4th quarter of 1968 and the 3rd quarter of 1971 to the 1st quarter of 1973 and that its average level fell considerably since the first oil shock.

We have seen that economic growth, the rate of growth of investment and the rate of profit all change in the same direction during the phases of business cycles. In fact, our definition of business cycles as a more profound phenomenon than mere fluctuations is this: in its upward phase, increase in investment demand drives the increase in aggregate demand, which in turn stimulates an increase in aggregate output, causing a rise in both the level of capacity utilization and the rate of profit. In contrast, in its downward phase of the business cycle, a decrease in investment demand forces the same variables to move in the opposite direction, *i.e.* to fall.

Figure 2.1 The Growth Rate of GNP (JAPAN)

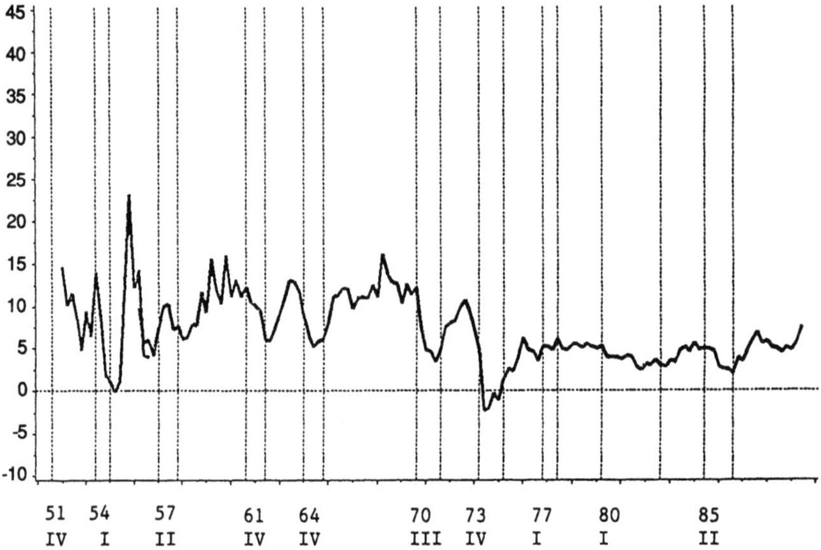

Figure 2.2 The Growth Rate of GNP and Investment (JAPAN)

solid curve: Investment
dotted curve: GNP

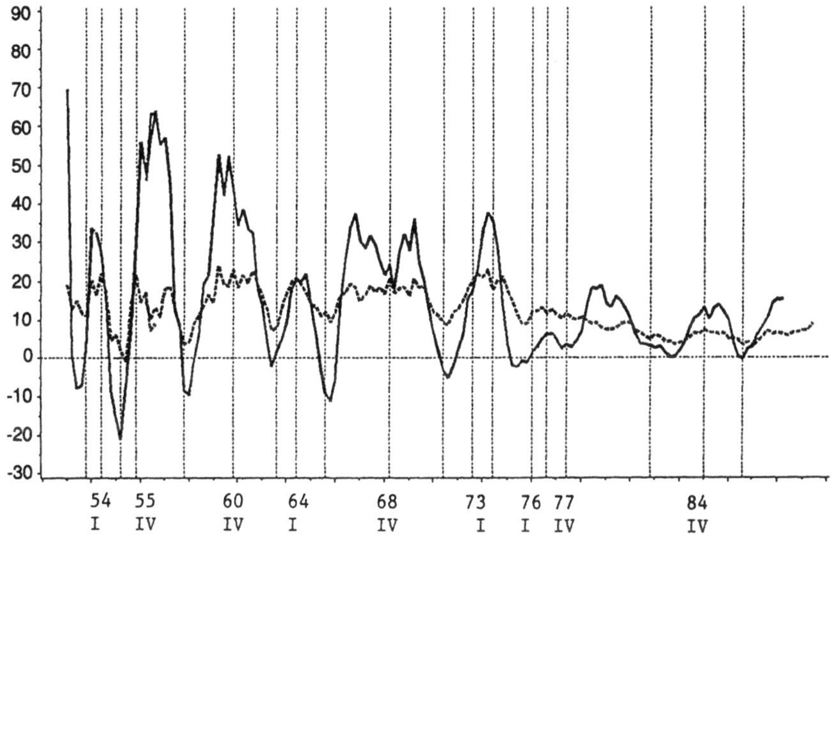

Figure 2.3 The Rate of Profit (JAPAN)

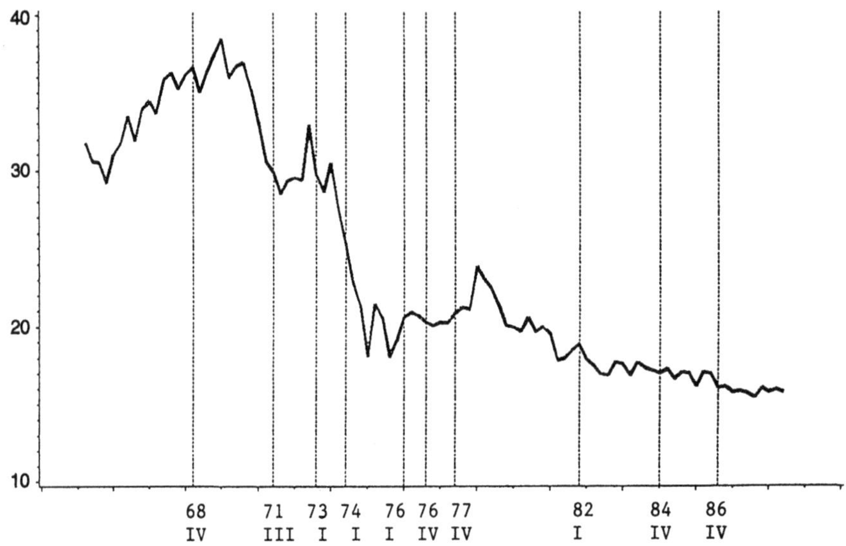

2.1.2 The Real Wages, Labour Productivity, and the Rate of Exploitation

We now turn to an examination of the implications of the business cycle for wage workers. It is evident that upward phases of business cycles are desirable periods for capitalists because of the favorable change in the rate of profit during these periods. But what about the conditions faced by wage workers during the periods? At first glance, it appears that workers are as happy as capitalists in the upward phases of business cycles because of increasing employment and wages. We examine next whether this is truly the case or not.

The upward phase of the business cycle is, as we have demonstrated, driven by increasing investment demand. During this phase how does consumption change? Figure 2.4 shows the ratio of investment to GNP (investment/GNP) and the ratio of consumption to GNP (consumption/GNP). It is obvious from the figure that they move in opposite directions. Their changes imply that in the upward phase of business cycles an increasingly large part of output is used for investment. Consequently, the share of output devoted to consumption shrinks. In downward phases the reverse is true.

Incidentally, a large portion of consumption is accounted for by wage workers. Therefore, provided that their propensity to consume does not change so much during phases of the business cycle, a rising consumption ratio in the upward phase means a falling share of wages in total income and vice versa. Figure 2.5 shows the share of wages in national income which, it can be seen, changes in line with the consumption ratio.

As the share of wages is defined as *real wages* × *employment* ÷ *real output*, the change in share of wages can be broken down into the changes in the real wages and labour productivity (real output/employment). As to their evolution through the phases of the business cycle, we note the following characteristics:

(1) The real wages rise in both upward and downward phases.

(2) In upward phases, labour productivity rises more rapidly than the real wages. Therefore the share of wages falls.

(3) In downward phases, labour productivity rises more slowly than the

real wage. Therefore the share of wages rises.

(4) Both the average rates of growth of real wages and labour productivity have dropped sharply since the first oil shock.

The real wages and labour productivity determine the degree of exploitation. In upward phases when the rate of growth of labour productivity outpaces the growth rate of real wages, the rate of exploitation rises and vice versa. During these phases surplus labour increases because the amount of labour which is employed to produce the consumer goods which wage workers buy back (necessary labour) decreases. This comes about because, despite the increasing quantities of consumer goods which wage workers purchase (*i.e.* rising real wages), the labour input per unit of consumer goods output is declining (rising labour productivity). Figure 2.5, which shows the share of wages, implies that the rate of exploitation goes up in the upward phases and goes down in the downward phases in business cycles. In this sense, wage workers are never happy in those periods when capitalists are happy.

It is a persistent belief that share of wages in total income goes up (*i.e.* the rate of exploitation goes down) in upward phases of business cycles. The rationale behind this is that the tight situation in the labour market forces the share of wages to rise. However, this argument overlooks the point that the commodity market is also in a tight situation. It is possible that the growth rate of money wages outpaces the growth rate of prices and therefore the real wages go up. However the growth rate of real wages is outpaced by the growth rate of labour productivity and therefore the share of wages goes down. This is a result of the basic feature of the upward phase of the business cycle which is that an increase in investment demand by capitalists drives the whole process.

Figure 2.4 Consumption/GNP, Investment/GNP (JAPAN)

solid curve: Investment/GNP
dotted curve: Consumption/GNP

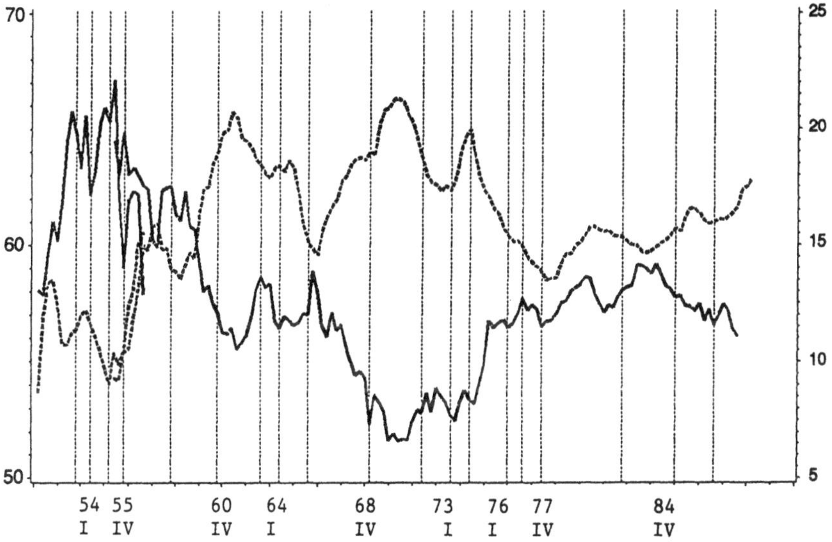

Figure 2.5 Share of Wages in Total Income (JAPAN)

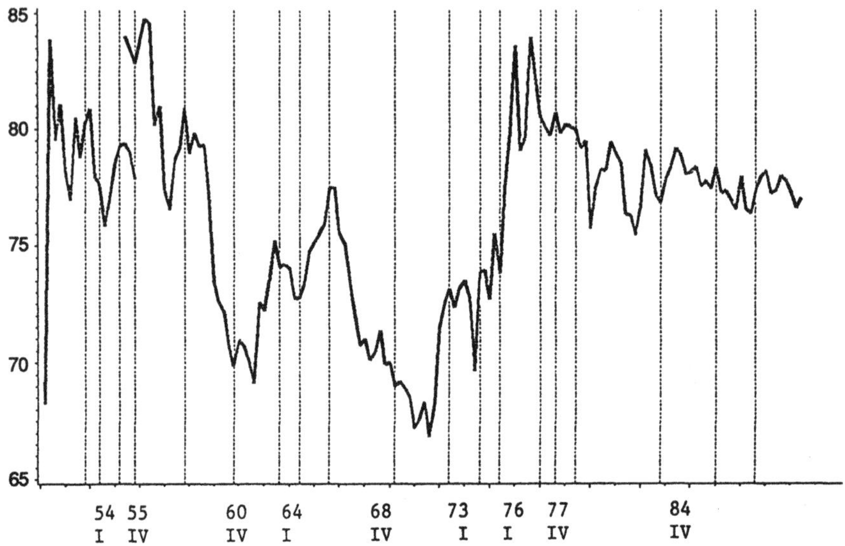

2.1.3 Fiscal Policy, Monetary Policy, and Foreign Trade

We can now examine government behavior and the external relations of an economy during the phases of the business cycle. First, let us consider fiscal policy. Figure 2.6 shows the ratio of government expenditure to GNP. It rises in the upward phases of business cycles and vice versa. As for its trans-cycle change, it continues to rise during 1970s and falls in 1980s.

Next, we turn to monetary policy. We examine the relationship between the official discount rate and the call rate which is an interest rate for borrowing between commercial banks. The call rate is considered to be an indicator of tightness in the financial market. Figure 2.7 clearly shows that the call rate changes in line with the official rate, which is fixed at high levels at late points in upward phases, especially *Jinmu* (the fourth quarter of 1955 to the second quarter of 1958), *Izanagi* (the first quarter of 1964 to the third quarter of 1965), the first quarter of 1974 to the first quarter of 1976 and the fourth quarter of 1977 to the first quarter of 1982. In contrast, it has been fixed at very low rates in the face of depressions, especially during the third quarter of 1971 to the first quarter of 1973, the fourth quarter of 1977 to the first quarter of 1982 and after the fourth quarter of 1984.

As it stands, although fiscal and monetary policy of the government are aimed at moderating or preferably doing away with entirely the cumulative movement of business cycles, we would point out that business cycles themselves have not disappeared.

Finally, we consider imports and exports. Figure 2.8 shows how the import ratio(import/GNP) and the export ratio(export/GNP) have changed in the postwar period. Examining the figure, we can see the following points are confirmed:

(1) There seems to be a structural change in the middle 1960s. Until then, in the upward phases of the business cycles increases in the import ratio exceed increases in the export ratio. Therefore, the excess export ratio (export/GNP − import/GNP) falls and in the late stage of booms it becomes negative. In depressions, although the export ratio falls, the import ratio drops more drastically. Therefore, the excess export ratio rises.

(2) Since 1965, exports exceed imports with the exception of the two oil shocks.

(3) Since the early 1970s, with the transformation of the international monetary system and the oil shocks, the amplitude of variation in the export and import ratios have become greater. This reflects the fact that international elements have grown more important in the Japanese economy.

In the United Kingdom (U.K.), as in Japan, the changes in the excess export ratio since the World War II move the opposite direction of the economic growth rate. In the U.S., there seems no regularity in its changes during the earlier portions of the same period. However, since the first oil shock the excess export ratio has followed the same pattern as Japan and the U.K.

It is interesting that the trends in the excess export ratios of these countries show big differences, reflecting their different statuses in the world economy. In the U.K., although the trend of its excess export ratio rises gradually, its average is negative. In the U.S., it falls and becomes negative in the 1980s.

To sum up, the growth rate of investment, its fraction of GNP, the rate of profit, employment, the growth rate of real wages and the growth rate of labour productivity change in line with the growth rate of the economy. In contrast, ratios of consumption, government expenditure and excess exports relative to GNP change differently.

Figure 2.6 Ratio of Government Expenditure to GNP (JAPAN)

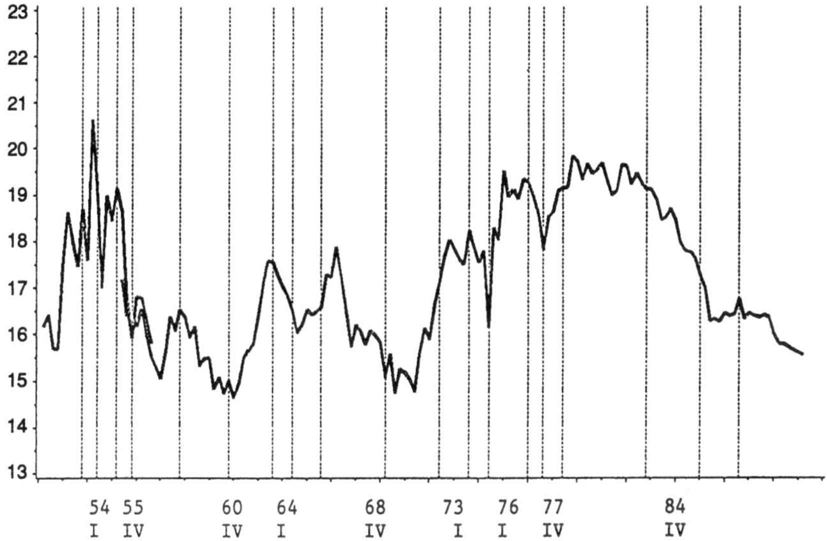

Figure 2.7 Call Rate, Official Rate (JAPAN)

solid curve: Call rate
dotted curve: Official rate

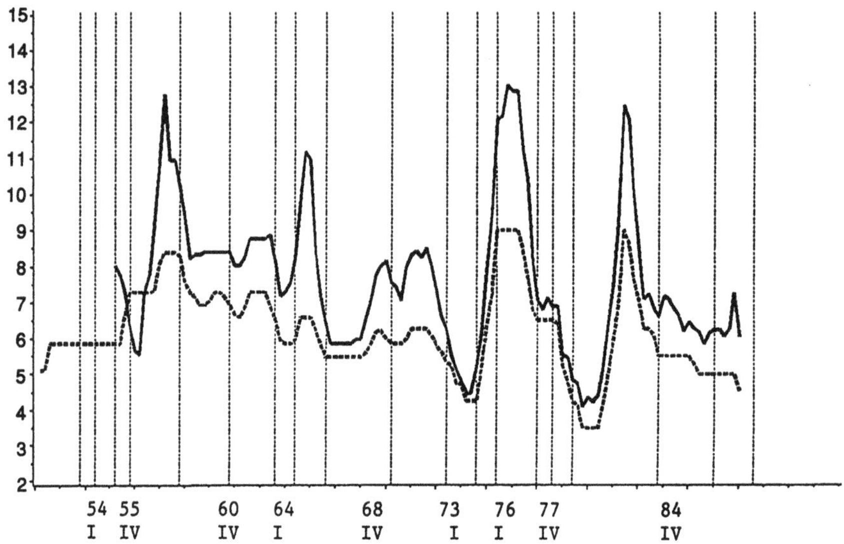

Figure 2.8 Import/GNP, Export/GNP, (Export – Import)/GNP (JAPAN)

solid curve: Export/GNP
dotted curve: Import/GNP
bar chart: (Export – Import)/GNP

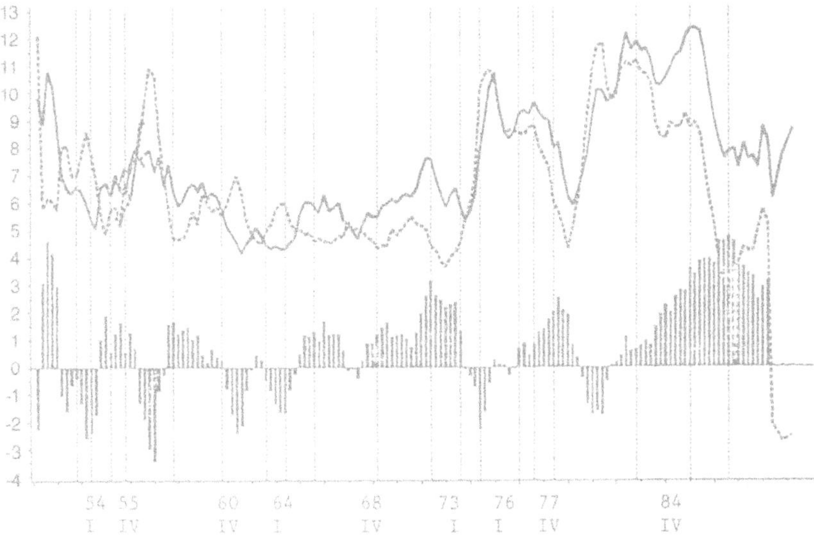

2.2 Trends

In this section, we explore the trends of fundamental economic variables over the long run.

2.2.1 The Growth Rate of Economy

As we have seen in part two of section one, capitalist economies experience cyclical movements. In booms, the demand for labour increases more rapidly than its supply, reducing unemployment. In contrast, depressions create unemployment. Through these cyclical movements, capitalist economies have realised economic growth over the long run. We choose the U.K. economy as an example to demonstrate the trends in the fundamental economic variables during the process of long run economic growth.

Table 2.2

period	*growth rate of labour supply*	*growth rate of productivity*	*growth rate of GNP*
1855 - 1965	0.4	0.6	1.0
1855 - 1913	0.5	0.7	1.2
1919 - 1938	0.0	0.9	0.9
1946 - 1965	0.3	1.0	1.3

Table 2.3

period	*growth rate of labour supply*	*growth rate of productivity*	*growth rate of GNP*
1953 - 1984	1.3	9.5	10.8
1953 - 1970	1.5	14.0	15.6
1970 - 1984	1.0	4.3	5.3

Figure 2.9 shows output, labour supply and employment in the long period from 1850 to 1970 with dashed lines indicating the two World Wars. It is impressive that output continues to increase far more rapidly than employment despite the disruptions the two World Wars. This signifies rising labour productivity. Also we notice that employment follows labour supply with temporary fluctuations. Therefore unemployment (labour supply – employment) fluctuates. But it neither increases or decreases cumulatively. We can separate economic growth into two factors: the growth of labour supply and the growth of labour productivity. Tables 2.2 and 2.3 show the results of estimates for the U.K. and Japan respectively. It is obvious that the growth of labour productivity contributed to economic growth more significantly than the growth of labour supply in both the U.K. and in Japan. Also it is obvious that the Japanese economic growth rate is higher than U.K.'s, and that the cause is not the difference in labour supply, but the higher growth rate of labour productivity in Japan. The long term rates of economic growth, which naturally differ according to countries and periods as they stand, are the axes of business cycles.

Figure 2.9 Supply of Labour, Employment, Output (U.K.)

solid curve: Supply of labour
dotted curve: Employment
bold curve: Output

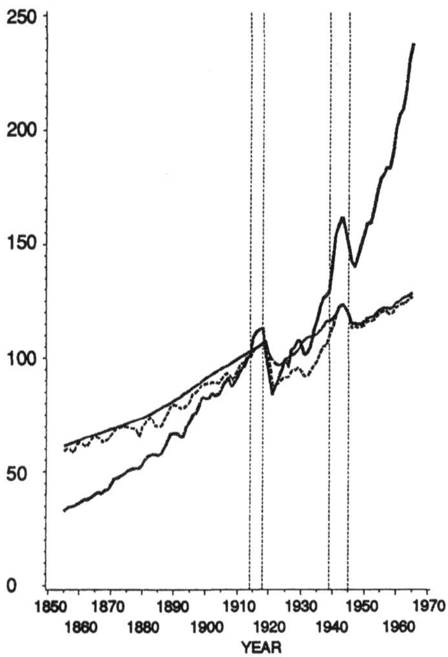

2.2.2 The Rate of Profit

The trend in the rate of profit has supreme implications for capitalist economies. If it falls, regardless of the cause, the capitalist economy faces a life or death crisis. Figure 2.10 shows the past performance of the U.K. rate of profit according to British statistics. As one can see, although it rises during each of the three periods separated by the two World Wars, the general trend over the whole period is for it to fall. The rate of profit is determined by two factors: the share of profit in total income and the ratio of capital to output as follows:

$$Rate\ of\ profit = \frac{profit}{capital} = \frac{profit}{output}\frac{output}{capital}. \tag{2.1}$$

Figure 2.11 shows how two factors have been changing. The coefficient of capital (capital/output) falls in each period and in the whole period as well. The share of wages (1 − profit/output) gradually rises in the whole period with the exception of the interwar period. These facts lead to the conclusion that the rate of profit fell in the whole period because of the rising share of wages despite the falling capital ratio. In fact, when the share of wages falls between the World Wars against its trend, the rate of profit rose sharply. The rise in the share of wages, which is observed in the downward phases of business cycles, is realised in the long run and causes the fall in the rate of profit.

We note that the cause of this fall in the rate of profit is different from one which Marx emphasized. In the British case, the rate of profit fell not because of a rising capital ratio but in spite of a falling one which corresponds to Marx's organic composition of capital. As labour productivity rises, which we have confirmed occurred in the British case, it seems that the technologies which are both labour and capital saving have been introduced. However, it appears that the rise in the real wages outweighed the positive effects these new technologies had on the rate of profit, leading finally to its fall. In Japan since the middle 1960s the rate of profit has fallen from above 30 percent to 20 percent with temporal fluctuations. This fall in the rate of profit has also been accompanied by a rise in the share of wages in the long run.

Figure 2.10 The Rate of Profit (U.K.)

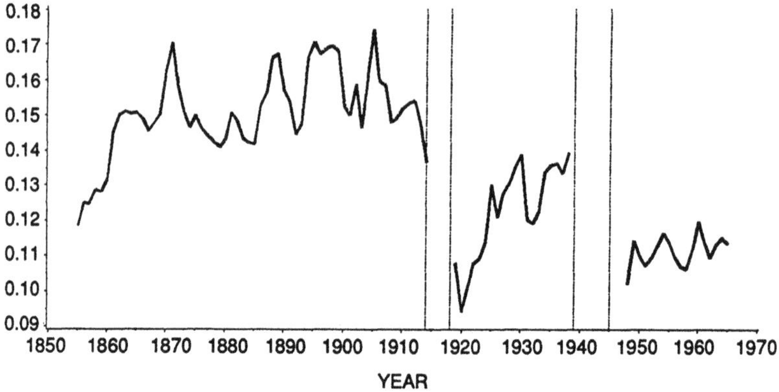

Figure 2.11 Capital Coefficient, Share of Wages (U.K.)

upper chart: Capital coefficient
lower chart: Share of wages

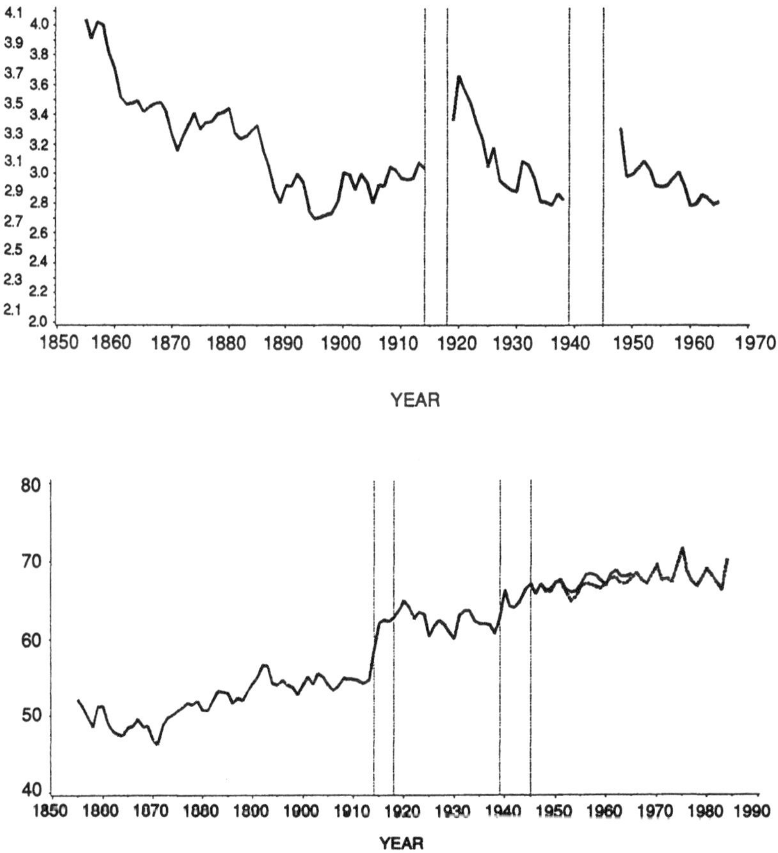

2.2.3 Monopoly Capital, Government and Wage Workers

An increase in the share of wages in total income is caused by a rise in the real wages which exceeds the growth of labour productivity. The rise in the real wages in turn is caused by the money wages rising faster than the price level. Figure 2.12 confirms these relations among prices, the money wages, the real wages and labour productivity, and also discloses the following information: (1) Prices (GNP deflator) fell in the late 1800s. (2) During the two World Wars, prices rose dramatically. (3) After the Second World War, a continuous rise in prices(inflation) is generated.

These facts are deeply related to such structural changes in capitalist economies as the increasing strength of wage workers, the development of monopoly capital and the intervention of the state in the economy.

Figure 2.13 shows the annual number of working days lost to industrial disputes as a result of the increasing strength of wage workers. It is clear that the trend is upward, but we can observe that it falls dramatically during periods of low economic growth and high unemployment such as the Great Depression and after the 1970s. Depressions when the growth rate of the economy and the rate of profit fall, are not only by all means hard time both for capitalists and for wage workers but also periods of total offensive of the former class against the latter one.

Figure 2.14 shows government expenditure as the share of GNP as one aspect of intervention of state into economy. It is very clear that its trend rises with epoches of the two World Wars. The change in monetary system (abolition of gold standard) to finance government expenditure and the increase in money supply caused continuous rise in prices (inflation). It is worth reminding that inflation and especially one in depressions (stagflation) are quite a strange phenomenon in the long perspective of capitalist development.

Figure 2.12(A) Money Income, Prices (U.K.)

solid curve: *per capita* Income from employment
dotted curve: GNP deflator

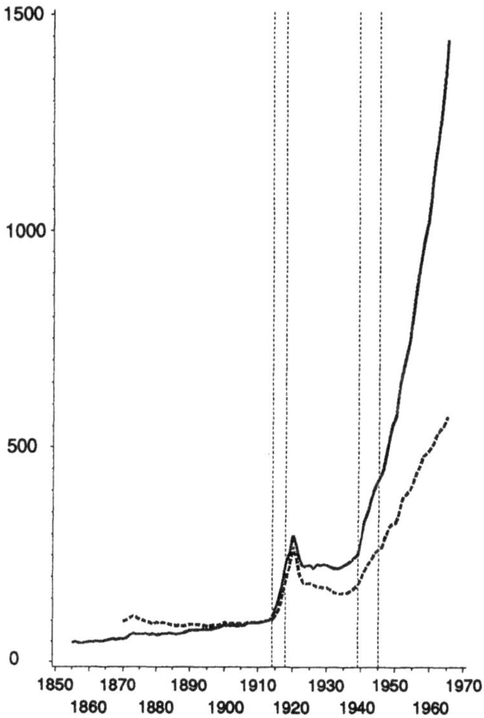

Figure 2.12(B) Real Wages and Labour Productivity (U.K.)

solid curve: Real wages
dotted curve: Labour productivity

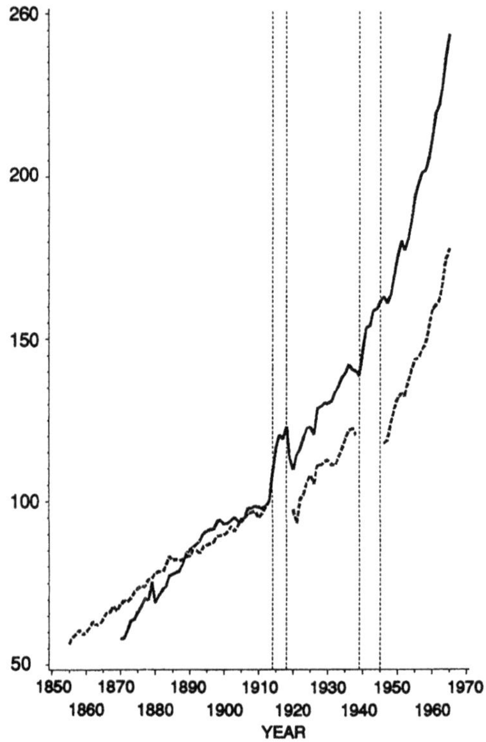

Figure 2.13 Working Days Lost (U.K.)

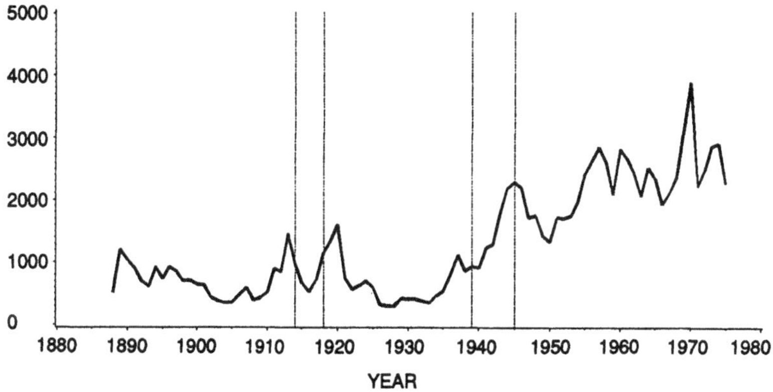

Figure 2.14 (Government Expenditure)/GNP (U.K.)

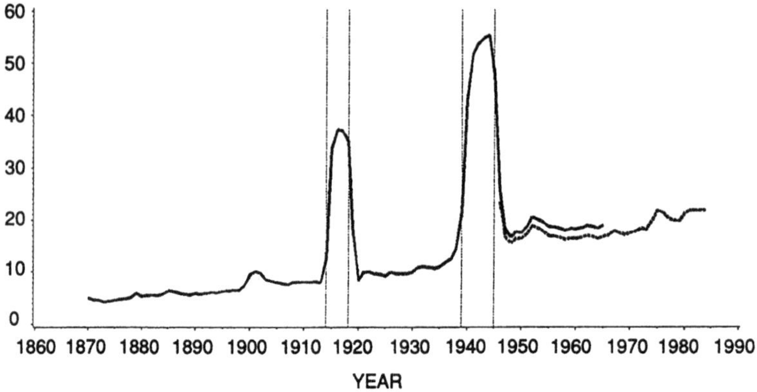

2.2.4 List of Definitions of Variables and Sources of Data

1. growth rate of economy

Japan: percent increase in GNP (at 1960, or 1980 prices, seasonally adjusted) on a year ago. *cf.* (J1), (J2) Table 4

U.K.: percent increase in GNP indicates (1980=100) on a year ago, *cf.*(B1) p.4, (B3) Table 8

2. growth rate of investment

Japan: percent increase in GNP at 1960, or 1980 prices on a year ago, *cf.* (J1), (J2) Table 4

3. investment ratio

Japan: gross domestic capital formation (equipment of private enterprises only)/GNE, *cf.* (J1), (J2)

4. consumption ratio

Japan: final consumption expenditure by households/GNP, *cf.* (J1), (J2)

5. rate of profit

Japan: (national income - compensation for employees)/capital stock of private enterprises, *cf.* (J1)

U.K.: (GDP - income from employment)/reproducible gross capital stock (at replacement cost), *cf.* (B3) Table 1, 46

6. real wages

Japan: (compensation for employees)/(number of employees/GNP deflator, *cf.* (J1), (J2)

U.K.: income from employment per capital/GDP deflator, *cf.* (B3) Table 1, 57, 61

7. labour productivity

Japan: GNP (at 1960, or 1980 prices) / number of workers engaged, *cf.* (J1), (J2)

U.K.: output-labour ratio (at constant prices), *cf.* (B3) Table 20

8. share of wages in total income

Japan: compensation for employees/(national income - income of private enterprises), *cf.* (J1), (J2)

U.K.: income from employment/(GDI-income from self employment), *cf.* (B2) various issues. income from employment/GDP, *cf.* (B3) Table 1

9. government expenditure ratio

Japan: (final government consumption expenditure)/GNP, *cf.* (J1), (J2).

U.K.: (final government consumption expenditure)/GDE, *cf.* (B1), (B2) and (B3) for data in the long run.

10. rate of interests

Japan: call rate and official interest rate, *cf.* (J1)

11. excess export ratio

Japan: (export – import+income from overseas-payment to overseas)/GNE, *cf.* (J1), (J2) Table 3

12. labour force, employment and output

U.K.: *cf.* (B3) Table 57

13. capital coefficient

U.K.: reproducible gross capital stock(at constant replacement cost)/GDP (at constant prices), *cf.* (B3) Table 20

14. industrial disputes

U.K.: *cf.* (B4)

Sources

Japan:
(J1) *NEEDS*, the Nihon Keizai Shimbun.
(J2) *Annual Report on National Account*, Economic Planning Agency, 1972.

the U.K.:

(B1) *Economic Trend: Annual Supplement*, Central Statistical Office, 1986.
(B2) *United Kingdom National Accounts*, Central Statistical Office, various issues.
(B3) Feinstein,C.H., *National Income, Expenditure and Output of the United Kingdom 1855-1965*, Cambridge University Press, 1972.
(B4) Mitchell,B.R., *European Historical Statistics*, Macmillan, 1981.

Chapter 3

Critical Survey of the Theories of Business Cycles

This chapter examines various types of business cycle theories. They can be divided into two major categories; orthodox or marxian. We can then further classify these theories into two types (Type I, II) according to whether they emphasize the so-called "the realization problem" or not.

Table 3.1 Types of Business Cycle theories

	TYPE I	*TYPE II*
Orthodox Theory	Theories of Hicks Kalecki, Kaldor and Harrod	Theories of Schumpeter and Hayek
Marxian Theory	Theories of Disproportionality or Underconsumption	Profit Squeeze Rising the Organic Composition

In this chapter we do not present the theories in the original forms in which their authors presented them. Instead, we have constructed a series of simple models that summarize the core of each theory and allow us to examine its dynamic properties. The results of these models are used to discuss the positive and negative aspects of each theory as an analytical tool for understanding the capitalist economy.

3.1 Marxian Theories of Crisis

Orthodox economics usually completes an analysis of the business cycle by attributing its existence to superficial causes (*e.g.* a low propensity to consume, a fall of the inducement of investment, the length of a gestation period, the durability of capital, a labour shortage and so on). We can classify these causes into two groups. One is closely related to the occurrence of crisis and is rooted in capitalist relations of production. The other is not directly related to the crisis in general. That is, the former includes such causes as a low propensity to consume and a fall in the inducement to invest. The technical ones, such as the gestation period of production and the durability of capital, belong in the latter group.

As examples of these sorts of business cycle causes, two cases, *i.e.* (1) a low propensity to consume and (2) the gestation period of production will be explained. As will be fully discussed below, a low propensity to consume is one of the important events which triggers a crisis. That the propensity to consume is low, however, is not based on a psychological law that people usually save. The reason for a low propensity to consume consists in the following facts: First, in a capitalist economy capitalists own all the means of production, and workers, who have no commodities except their own labour power, are exploited. Secondly, not all of the surplus products which are expropriated through exploitation re-consumed. As the gestation period of production becomes longer, capitalists have to determine the level of production according to their expectations of the circumstances of a more distant future. These expectations are often mistaken and a crisis is generated. Though the gestation period of production is, in a certain sense, determined technically, the reason why it becomes a cause of a crisis is that profit motivated capitalists determine the level of production, the level of investment and other important factors privately and separately.

As Marx himself did not develop a full crisis theory, and scattered various ideas concerning crises throughout *Capital*, many types of crisis theory have been presented. As already stated above, we organize these into two categories (Type I and Type II).

The theories which belong under Type I assume that all commodities produced can necessarily be sold, in other words, they abstract away from the analysis of effective demand. And they demonstrate that the causes which would lower the rate of profit are powerful enough to lead to crisis. Some contend that the rate of profit must fall because of the rising organic composition of capital (M.Dobb and so on). Others insist that rising real wage rates reduce the rate of profit (K.Marx, K.Uno, *etc.*).

The Type II theories emphasize the importance of the so-called realization problem. That is, they examine the factors which reduce the effective demand for the commodities. The Type II theories can be divided into two subgroups. One is known as "The Theory of Disproportionality Between Sectors"(Tugan-Baranowsky, Hilferding), and the other is "The Underconsumptionist Theory"(Sismondi, Malthus, Sweezy). We now turn to a detailed discussion of each of the above theories.

3.1.1 Type I Theories of Crisis

In a capitalist economy capitalists have control over the primary decisions on production. The search for profits is the decisive motive in capitalists' production decisions, and they accumulate capital in order to acquire further profits. Accordingly, they lower the levels of production and investment when the actual rate of profit happens to be less than their expected rate of profit. It is essential for the analysis of business cycles to focus on the movement of the rate of profit. The Type I theories do not connect the fall of the rate of profit with a shortage of effective demand for commodities, but instead they emphasize such factors as "the rising organic composition of capital" and "the rising real wage rate".

Rising Real Wage Rate Leads to a Falling Rate of Profit

For example, the chain of ideas in Uno's crisis theory[1] is: a labour shortage in a boom $\Rightarrow$ a rising real wage rate $\Rightarrow$ a fall in the rate of profit $\Rightarrow$ a fall in the rate of accumulation. Therefore, we call this type of theory a "Rising Real Wage Rate Leads to a Falling Rate of Profit" type model. To simplify the discussion, we assume a one-sector economy where no technical change occurs. At the beginning of period t there exists a labour force, L_t,

[1] cf. K.Uno, *Principles of Political Economy - Theory of a Purely Capitalist Society -*, Harvester Press, 1977.

and a collection of capital equipment, K_t, which has been accumulated by capitalists. The production function is assumed to be as follows:

$$X_t = \sigma K_t, \tag{3.1}$$

$$N_t = nX_t. \tag{3.2}$$

As we abstract away from technical change, the coefficients remain constant. In this "Rising Real Wage Rate Leads to a Falling Rate of Profit" type model the existing capital equipment is assumed to be fully utilized at all times. When the quantity of capital is equal to K_t, the output produced is σK_t and the labour which is necessary to produce it is $n\sigma K_t$ (which equals N_t). If we suppose that the labour supply, L_t, grows at a constant rate, ν, then $L_t = (1+\nu)L_{t-1}$ and the rate of employment is defined as N_t/L_t. The level of the rate of employment indicates the tightness of the labour market. The essential point of this model is that the real wage rate of period t is supposed to be determined by the rate of employment of the same period. This relationship is formalized as follows:

$$\frac{R_t - R_{t-1}}{R_{t-1}} = \omega(\frac{N_t}{L_t} - e^*), \qquad \omega, e^* : const. \tag{3.3}$$

For instance, if the value of response coefficient, ω, is 0.25 and that of the critical rate of employment, e^*, is 0.8, then the growth rate of the real wage rate equals 2.5% in which case the rate of employment in this period is 0.9. This equation is often referred to as a "Bargaining Equation" because it formalizes the idea that the bargaining power of labour becomes stronger as the labour market becomes tighter. We can say that Marx himself shared this idea.[2] If the actual rate of employment exceeds the critical rate of employment, the real wage rate rises faster, and, conversely, if it falls below the critical employment rate, then the growth rate of the real wage rate becomes negative and declines.

We assume that workers completely consume their wages and save nothing. Furthermore, for the simplicity of discussion, it is assumed that

[2] "Taking them as a whole, the general movements of wages are exclusively regulated by the expansion and contraction of the industrial reserve army, and this in turn corresponds to the periodic alternations of the industrial cycle." *Capital*, vol. I, p.790.

the capital equipment never depreciates. If output is defined as X_t, then the capitalists acquire the profits $(X_t - R_tN_t)$. As they necessarily invest the total profits, the supply and demand for output always coincides and the "realization problem" cannot occur. In other words, the level of investment is determined such that equilibrium in the commodity market can be achieved. Accordingly, the equation below holds:

$$X_t = R_tN_t + I_t. \tag{3.4}$$

In the case where the wage is paid post factum, the rate of profit can be calculated by:

$$r_t = \frac{X_t - R_tN_t}{K_t}. \tag{3.5}$$

As easily seen from the above equation, the rate of profit is equal to the rate of accumulation (I_t/K_t). During the period t, it is accumulated and the quantity of capital, at the beginning of the period $t+1$, increases to $K_t + I_t$.

As has been stated above, K_{t+1}, R_t and L_{t+1} are endogenously determined and the same process is repeated again and again. Given the parameters σ, n, ω, e^* and ν, the movement of the seven fundamental economic variables (output, employment, capital equipment, real wage rate, investment, labour supply and the rate of profit) are determined by the above model.

If we assume that the initial rate of employment is equal to e^*, and the initial real wage rate takes a value which equalizes the rate of accumulation and the growth rate of the labour supply (ν), then the rate of employment always remains equal to e^* and the rate of profit is equal to the constant ν.[3] However, how does the system respond when the initial rate of employment

[3]The growth rate of employment is as follows:

$$\frac{N_{t+1} - N_t}{N_t} = \sigma(1 - nR_t).$$

The growth rate of employment is equal to the rate of accumulation (the rate of profit). If the initial rate of employment is equal to e^* and the growth rate of labour supply is equal to that of labour demand, the rate of employment remains e^*. This condition can be satisfied

and the real wage rate do not take the specific values stated above? The results of a computer simulation of this situation is depicted in Figure 3.1. This figure demonstrates that this system generates regular cyclical movements. To sum up, we conclude that the "Rising Real Wage Rate Leads to a Falling Rate of Profit" model, is capable of reproducing the regular cyclical movements seen in actual capitalist economies.

We divide the business cycle into four phases according to the movement of the rate of accumulation, and analyze the characteristics of each phase. By doing so, we can explain why economies regularly fluctuate between booms and depressions.

We begin with the recovery phase of the cycle (the period 1-2 in Figure 3.1). During this period the level of the rate of accumulation is low but is rising. The prosperity phase (2-3) sees an accumulation rate that is high and rising. Next, is the period when the boom ends and the crisis occurs (3-4). At this time, the level of the accumulation rate is high but falling. The final phase is depression (4-1): The level of the accumulation rate is low and falling.

---

if the initial value of real wage rate R_0 is as follows:

$$\sigma(1 - nR_0) = \nu,$$

or

$$R_0 = \frac{\sigma - \nu}{\sigma n}.$$

Conversely, the real wage rate remains constant if the rate of employment continue top take the value e^*. In this case, however, the inequality $\sigma - \nu > 0$ must be hold. In the following, we assume that this inequality is satisfied.

Figure 3.1 The movement of the rate of accumulation, real wage rate and the rate of employment

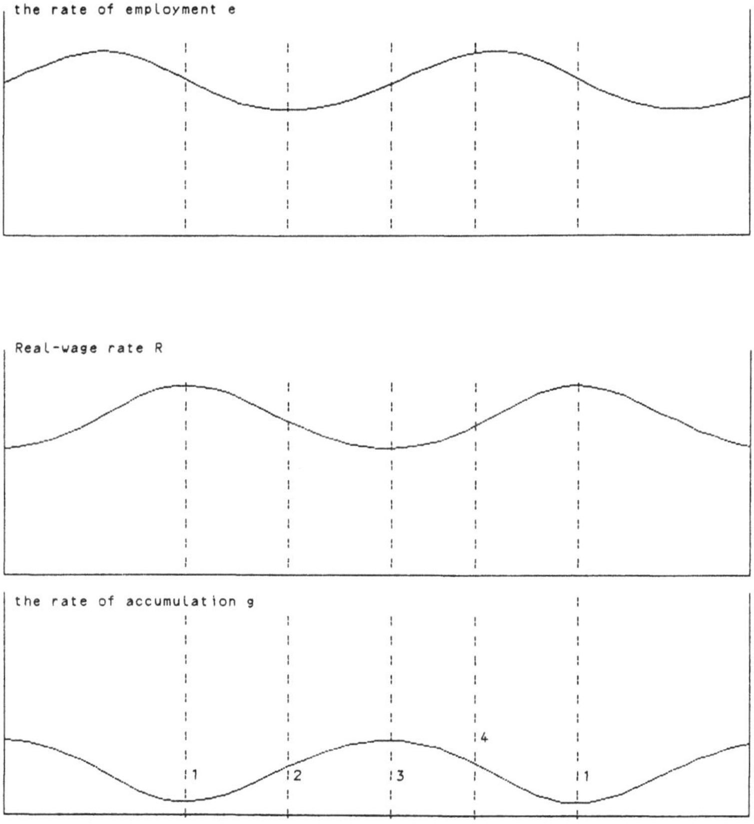

As the real wage rate is high in the period of recovery, profits are squeezed and the rate of accumulation remains at a low level. Therefore, the growth rate of employment is low and below the growth rate of the labour supply. That is, the rate of unemployment rises gradually. As the bargaining power of labour is inversely related to the rate of unemployment, the real wage rate begins to decline. This decline of the real wage rate furnishes an increase in the profits of capitalists and the rate of accumulation. In these circumstances, the business cycle heads steadily upward and the rate of accumulation is rising. When investment proceeds steadily, capital equipment is accumulated and the demand for labour, which is necessary to utilize the machines, increases. At this point, the growth rate of labour demand exceeds the growth rate of labour supply. However, so many remain unemployed that the real wage rate continues to fall because the rate of employment is still below the critical value e^*. But the difference between the actual rate of employment and e^* has become smaller, so the speed of the real wage decline begins to slow. As accumulation proceeds further, the actual rate of employment exceeds the critical value e^*. At the same time, the real wage rate begins to rise and conversely the rate of profit and the rate of accumulation begins to fall. The level of the rate of accumulation is still high, the growth rate of labour demand is also high and the real wage rate rises further.

As the rate of accumulation goes down, the growth rate of labour demand tends to be below that of labour supply and the industrial reserve army appears again. Though the number of unemployed workers increases and the rate of employment falls, the real wage rate continues to rise as long as the rate of employment exceeds the value e^*. In such a case, the rate of accumulation continues to fall, the demand for labour falls, and finally the rate of employment reaches e^*.

The above sketch shows why the economy undergoes cyclical movements. Unless the economy experiences some external shocks, it habitually repeats the same cyclical movements. As we abstract away from the existence of technical change, the cyclical movement of the growth rate of output is the same as that of capital accumulation. As long as the level of real wage rate is below the level of labour productivity $(1/n)$, the rate of accumulation must be positive. So the absolute level (not the growth rate) of output, capital equipment and employment increases cyclically. Through the cyclical movements such situations as "(i) the growth rate of output and capital is equal to that of labour supply and (ii) the rate of unemployment, real wage rate and the rate of profit continues to be constant value" could be realized in the long-run on average. Here both the rate of unemployment and the real wage rate exhibit downward movements and the rate of profit does not decline. From these facts one should think that these economic state are very harmonious for capitalists and workers. But that is not necessarily right. The reason why this is so is explained as follows. As long as the growth rate of capital equipment is positive, the material wealth in the form of capital equipment is accumulated by capitalists. On the contrary, workers are paid wages by which they can only maintain their standards of living as before.

At the core of this type of theory is the idea of class conflict between capitalists and workers. The change of the power relationship between the two classes, which was specified as the "bargaining equation", endogenously generates regular cycles. This is the fundamental characteristic of this model. The model can be evaluated as a constructive theory on the grounds that it theorizes the contradictory features of a capitalist economy as a system. That is, the capitalist economy cannot survive without labour that capitalists themselves cannot produce. A few more words are appropriate on this point.[4]

Some have criticised the "Rising Real Wage Rate Leads to a Falling Rate of Profit" type model by pointing to the fact that it explains the cause of a crisis as arising from an exogenous factor (the limit of the labour supply), and they consider it therefore as merely a superficial theory. Such criticism seems irrelevant. It is irrelevant because it is indispensable for a capitalistic economy to ensure a steady supply of "labour power as a commodity", and it is also a very capitalistic phenomenon that the rate of accumulation declines when the rate of profit falls.

The first drawback of this type of theory consists in how it formulates the mechanism which determines investment and the real wage rate. As was stated before, to abstract away from the realisation problem or to assume

[4]The mathematical formulation of the model above is the same as Goodwin's. And we think that the implication of his model consists in this point. *cf.* R.M.Goodwin, "A Growth Cycle", in C.H.Feinstein (ed.) *Socialism, Capitalism and Economic Growth,* Cambridge, 1967.

the existence of a Say's Law implies that the profits which capitalists gain will be reinvested automatically. It abstracts away from, so to speak, the "independent" investment activity of capitalists and the "independence of accumulation demand" in a capitalist economy. Accordingly, it could be termed a theory of the capitalist economy without capitalists.

The ideas of this theory may have derived from the way the originators interpreted the theoretical significance of Marx's *Reproduction Scheme.*[5] They understood that the equilibrium relationships of the Reproduction Scheme can be realized by the smooth working of the price mechanism. Though the theory can be classified as marxian, such ideas about smooth workings of price mechanisms bear a strong resemblance to neoclassical theory.

The second drawback is related to the movement of the real wage rate. In this model, when the rate of unemployment falls, the real wage rate necessarily rises and the rate of profit declines. But it is the money wage rate that is regulated by the tightness of a labour market. And it is not the real wage rate, but the money wage rate that is determined by the bargaining between capitalists and workers. As the real wage rate is the money wage rate divided by the price level, the movement of the real wage rate is influenced not only by supply and demand on the labour market, but also by the conditions in the commodity market. If we take into consideration that the workers are aware of both the level of the money wage rate and the level of prices when they sit at the negotiating table, we can reinterpret the bargaining equation as an equation for making a claim on the real wage rate. But we must note that even in that case stated above, the real wage rate claimed by workers cannot necessarily be realised.

3.1.2 Type II Theories of Crisis

Here, the underconsumption theory, which could be regarded as the major Type II theory, will be discussed. Underconsumption theory, conceived of in a broad sense, has a long history and there seems to be many variants of it. In fact, we could call Lauderdale, an early 19th century economist,

[5]See Y.Sato, "Marx-Goodwin Growth Cycle in a Two Sector Economy", *Zeitschrift für Nationökonomie*, 1985.

as the first underconsumptionist.[6] In this school of thought we find such famous economists as Sismondi, Malthus, Rosa Luxemburg and Sweezy.

Although many have discussed the fundamental propositions of underconsumption theory, it has seemed to be very difficult to construct a mathematical model that could be regarded as an underconsumptionist one.[7] So we have undertaken the task to construct a model which emphasizes some aspects of underconsumption theory and analyzes its dynamic properties.

By the way, in the following pages, we should abstract the theories of "accumulation impossible"(Sismondi, Malthus) which bases on the underconsumption of workers. Actually in capitalist economy workers are exploited and their level of consumption is very low. On the other hand the consumption demand of capitalist cannot be so high because they have to reinvest most of their profit to maintain their existence as capitalist. From these reasons Malthus discussed that the demand for commodities are very restricted in a capitalist economy and there is always possible over-production. If there is no demand of the "third" except capitalists and workers, it is impossible for the economy to extend their production. But the view that connects the underconsumption of workers directly to the occurrence of crisis is false because they miss the point that capitalists buy commodities for the consumption purpose and at the same time they buy capital goods for replacement and accumulation.[8]

To make it clear, we abstract away from the consumption of capitalists and the saving of workers. The demand for commodities consists only of the accumulation demand of capitalists and the consumption demand of workers. If the underconsumption of workers can be a major cause which triggers a crisis, the argument should be developed as follows: in the boom the consumption demand of labour falls gradually, it reduces the aggregate demand for commodities and it ultimately triggers a crisis. As the consumption demand of workers is the product of the real wage rate and employment, we have to demonstrate that the real wage rate and/or employment falls in the course of a boom. If we cannot establish this, we

[6] *cf.* M.F.Bleaney, *Underconsumption Theories - A History and Critical Analysis -*, International Publishers, 1976, p.18.

[7] "It is difficult to summarise these theories because, with some notable exceptions, their scientific standard is lower than the standard of those reviewed earlier in this volume." *cf.* G.Harberler, *Prosperity and Depression*, United Nations 3rd ed. 1952, p.119.

[8] T.R.Malthus, *Principles of Political Economy*, 1820.

cannot say that consumption demand falls as the boom proceeds.

We have constructed two models of these views. The first model, which stresses the fall of employment, is called the "Rising Productivity of Labour Leads to Falling Consumption Demand" model and the second, which stresses the decline of the real wage rate, is called the "Falling Real Wage Rate Leads to Falling Consumption Demand" model.

Rising Productivity of Labour Leads to a Falling Consumption Demand

If pressed, we would admit that this type of underconsumption model bears a resemblance to the work of P. M. Sweezy.[9] While the real wage rate of workers is lowered, capitalists invest most of their profits, and constant capital becomes larger and larger and production capacity expands. That is, the theory declares that the growth rate of accumulation tends to be larger than the growth rate of aggregate demand for commodities, because a tendency towards underconsumption is immanent in a capitalist economy.

Let us imagine an economy where the real wage rate is equal to the constant R_0 and the production capacity expands unceasingly as a result of the rising of labour productivity. The equilibrium condition of commodity market is given as:

$$X_t = R_0 N_t + I_t. \tag{3.6}$$

But this equation does not mean that there exists a demand for commodities which ensures the full utilization of capital equipment. It is important to grasp that this sort of thinking is opposed entirely to that of Rising Real Wage Rate Leads to a Falling Rate of Profit type model. In fact, a disequilibrium always occurs in a commodity market because in a capitalist economy there is no one who controls the entire economic system, and individual capitalists decide on the level of production, employment and investment based on their private view. The question is how to understand the nature of this disequilibrium. The disequilibrium can be seen as either *(i)* the commodities produced are greater than the demand (*i.e.* after the

[9] *cf. The Theory of Capitalist Development*, 1942, Chap.10 Realization Crisis.

production the commodities are excess), or *(ii)* the commodities produced are equal to demand but the capital equipment is underutilized.
Here we assume the disequilibrium is type *(ii)* and we will express that as the change of the rate of utilization of capital. If σ units of a commodity can be produced when one unit of capital equipment is utilized under normal conditions, the degree of utilization can be defined as:

$$\delta_t = \frac{X_t}{\sigma K_t}, \qquad \sigma : const. \tag{3.7}$$

Next, as n_t unit of labour is assumed to be necessary to produce one unit of a commodity, the equilibrium condition can be expressed as:

$$(1 - n_t R_0)\sigma\delta_t = \frac{I_t}{K_t} \equiv g_t. \tag{3.8}$$

In addition, labour productivity is supposed to grow at a constant rate. So the movements of this model are determined if we specify an investment function for capitalists. On this point, we suppose that capitalists determine the rate of accumulation (I/K) at the same rate as the previous period if the rate of utilization is equal to unity, that is, the capital equipment is normally utilized in the previous period, at a greater rate if over utilized, and at a lesser rate if under utilized. Accordingly, the investment function is:

$$g_{t+1} = g_t + \beta(\delta_t - 1), \qquad \beta > 0 : const. \tag{3.9}$$

The movement of the rate of accumulation in this economy is shown in Figure 3.2.[10] Curve A, which is upward sloping, expresses the relationship between labour productivity and the rate of accumulation when capital equipment is utilized normally. The line above curve A indicates that the capital equipment is over utilized, and the line which is below it means that it is under utilized (there exists idle capacity).

[10] If the value of β is 0.01, the economy moves on the upper cumulative disequilibrium path. On the contrary, if its value is 0.005, the economy runs into the depression.

Figure 3.2 The movement of the rate of accumulation

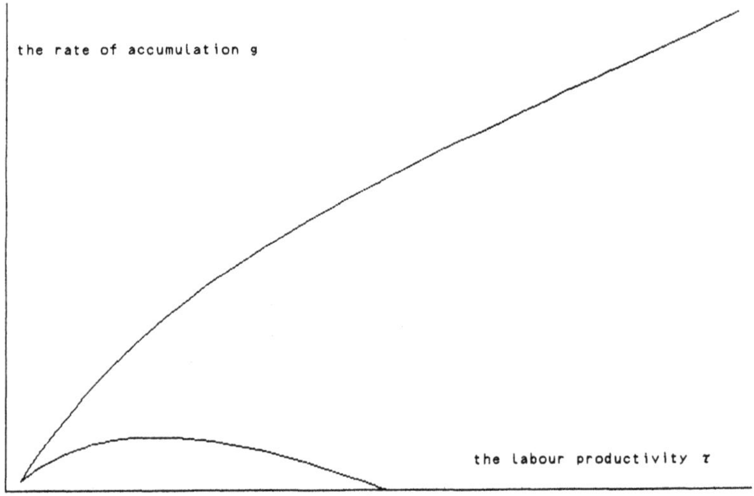

The problem that we have to discuss here is whether the boom slows down or not. In Figure 3.2 two loci, which are supposed to be the initial point of the boom are depicted. And they have the same initial values for the rate of accumulation and labour productivity but the investment behavior of capitalists is different (that is, the response to the change in the rate of utilization differs). As easily can be seen from Figure 3.2, the boom necessarily slows down in the Rising Productivity of Labour Leads to a Falling Consumption Demand" type model. The upward cumulative process of disequilibrium continues in the case that the response to the change of the rate of utilization is large enough (*i.e.*, the coefficient β is very large), though the extent of the over utilization of capital is the same. The reason why the economy could maintain the upward movement can be explained by two effects which are related to consumption demand. One is the negative effect that is described as the relationship: a rise in labour productivity $\Rightarrow$ a fall in employment $\Rightarrow$ a fall in consumption demand. And the other is a positive effect that is in the relationship: a rise of accumulation demand $\Rightarrow$ a rise of output $\Rightarrow$ a rise of employment $\Rightarrow$ an increase of consumption demand.

If the latter effect exceeds the former as in the case of a large β, consumption demand can increase. Conversely, in the case where β is small, the latter effect is less powerful than the former and the boom ceases.

We conclude that the underconsumption of workers may be one of the causes which slows down the economy, but in spite of the existence of underconsumption, prosperity can continue in certain circumstances. From this point of view we may say that the theory of underconsumption specified here can be appraised as a theory that demonstrates "one possible cause" of crises.

Falling Real Wage Rate Leads to a Falling Consumption Demand

The causal relationship of the Falling Real Wage Rate Leads to a Falling Consumption Demand type model is summarized as follows: prosperity $\Rightarrow$ a fall in the real wage rate $\Rightarrow$ a fall of consumption demand $\Rightarrow$ a fall of the aggregate demand $\Rightarrow$ a depression. In Uno's theory it is the "rise" of the real wage rate that slows down business, but in this model it is the "fall" of the real wage rate which causes the downturn. On this point, this model is in strong contrast with Uno's theory. The important aspect of this model to explain is how the real wage rate falls as the cyclical upswing proceeds.

Up to the present, we have not explicitly discussed the claim that the behavior of capitalists in determining the level of production and investment, however,they are supposed to require a certain level of the rate of profit. And if the required rate of profit is assumed to depend on the rate of accumulation, it rises in the boom with the rate of accumulation and so the real wage rate falls. This reasoning stated above is the fundamental idea of "the Falling Real Wage Rate Leads to – Falling the consumption demand" type model.

Assume that capitalists determine the required rate of profit of period t with reference to the realized rate of accumulation in the period $t-1$. The required rate of profit will be higher, the higher the rate of accumulation. Since the investment fund is mainly supplied by undistributed profits, when more investment funds are necessary for high accumulation, the required rate of profit is correspondingly high. Accordingly, we could assume that the required rate of profit is an increasing function of the rate of accumulation. That is:

$$r_t^* = \phi(g_{t-1}) \tag{3.10}$$

where $\phi\prime > 0$, r^* is "the required rate of profit". On the other hand, when the production technique is such that:

$$\begin{aligned} X_t &= \delta_t \sigma K_t, \qquad \sigma : const. && (3.11) \\ N_t &= n X_t, \qquad n : const. && (3.12) \end{aligned}$$

the realized rate of profit is expressed as:

$$r_t = \sigma\delta_t(1 - nR_t).$$

If capitalists want to obtain the required rate of profit with normal utilization of capital equipment, they have to set a price which satisfies the relationship:

$$p = \frac{r^* p K_t}{X_t} + wn \tag{3.13}$$

$$price = (the\ required\ profit\ margin) + (wage\ cost)$$

That the required rate of profit can be realized under the normal utilization of capital means that the equation below is satisfied:

$$r_t^* = \sigma(1 - nR_t). \tag{3.14}$$

The price equation above is rewritten version of this equation. As can be easily seen, the price setting equation is nothing else but "the Fullcost Principle."

Therefore, we conclude that *(i)* the actual (realized) rate of profit is above (below) the required rate of profit when the rate of utilization of capital is above (below) the normal level and *(ii)* the real wage rate falls when the required rate of profit rises.

As for the accumulation behavior of capitalists, we assume it is the same as in the Rising Productivity of Labour Leads to Falling Consumption Demand model.

What are the characteristics of the dynamic movements which come out of an oligopolistic economy where capitalists can pursue their desired level of profits? First, the rate of utilization of capital is equal to unity, the rate of accumulation and the real wage rate are constant in the initial period, and will thereafter maintain the same value as long as the initial rate of accumulation and the real wage rate take the precise values of g^* and R^* respectively. These are given as:

$$g^* = \phi(g^*) \tag{3.15}$$

$$R^* = \frac{1}{n}(1 - \frac{g^*}{\sigma}). \tag{3.16}$$

The first equation indicates that the capital equipment is utilized at normal level, and the second equation means that the real wage rate is such that the required rate of profit which corresponds to the specific rate of accumulation g^* can be realized. Therefore, if the initial rate of accumulation is equal to g^*, there is no reason for capitalists to change it.

Next we turn to the question of what sort of dynamic behavior the economy exhibits when the initial rate of accumulation and real wage rate differ from g^* and R^*. Assume that the economy is in such a phase that the degree of utilization of capital exceeds unity and the rate of accumulation is rising. The rise in the rate of accumulation increases the accumulation demand and at the same time raises the required rate of profit, which lowers the real wage rate. After all, the change in the degree of utilization depends on both factors. One is a positive effect that the increase in accumulation raises the degree of utilization. The other is a negative effect that the rise in the required rate of profit lowers the real wage rate, and consequently lowers consumption demand which lowers the degree of utilization. If the former effect exceeds the latter, the degree of utilization rises and vice versa. How the real wage rate falls depends on the behavior of capitalists in pursuing the required rate of profit. Here, we simulate the model in the case that the required function is in the form:

$$r_t^* = m_1 g_{t-1} + m_0, \qquad m_1 > 0 : const. \tag{3.17}$$

The result of the simulation is shown as in Figure 3.3. The straight line A, which is downward sloping, expresses the combination of the rate of accumulation, g^*, and the real wage rate, R^*, which ensures the normal utilization of capital. The area which is above line A expresses the over utilization of capital equipment, and the area which is below line A expresses the under utilization of productive capacity. In Figure 3.3 two loci are depicted that have the same initial values but differ in the value of m_1 (the reaction coefficient of the function above).

Figure 3.3 The movement of the rate of accumulation

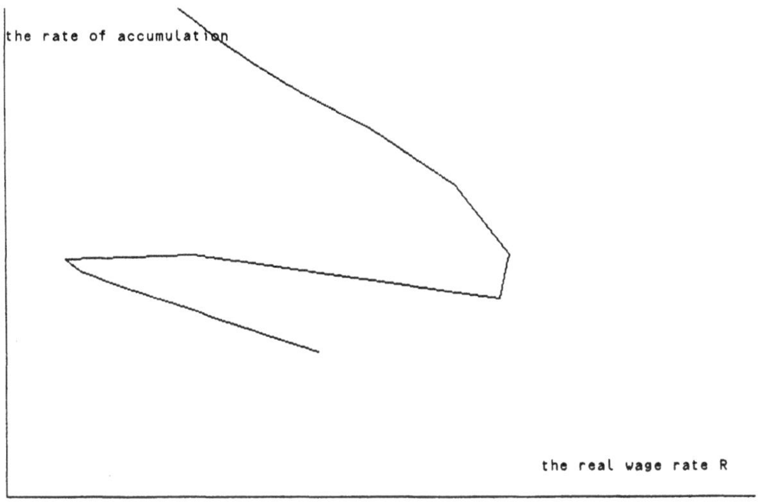

If the requirement of capitalists for profits is strong (*i.e.* m_1 is large), and the negative effect of a rise in the rate of accumulation on the real wage rate is large, the degree of utilization falls. Even if the level of capital utilization falls, the rate of accumulation can rise as long as the utilization level exceeds the normal level. But, since the negative effect is so strong, the degree of utilization of capital falls to less than the normal level and the economy begins to slow down.

If the requirement of capitalists for profits is not so strong (*i.e.* m_1 is small), the negative effect of a rise in the rate of accumulation is not large. In such a case, both the direct positive effect of a rise of accumulation and the indirect positive effect on consumption demand, caused by increasing employment, exceed the negative effect stated above. Accordingly, the upward movement of the economy continues.[11]

What was said about the Rising Productivity of Labour Leads to Falling Consumption Demand model is relevant here. That is, the underconsumption of wage workers can be assessed as "one possible moment" which could trigger a crisis.

Until now we have stated that the underconsumption of workers cannot be considered the only cause a crisis, but we should not underestimate the relationship between the underconsumption of workers and crises. Accumulation demand functions as a major determinant of aggregate demand and the unstable character of accumulation demand produces cyclical movements in a capitalist economy. Since the viability of the capitalist economy rests on the existence of exploitation of workers, the consumption demand of workers alone cannot account for all of the commodities produced. Even when accumulation demand falls, overproduction does not occur and/or the economy does not rush into crisis in the event that a rise in the consumption demand of workers can cancel out the decline in accumulation demand. With this in mind, we conclude that without the underconsumption of workers, accumulation demand cannot play a determinate role in the economy and the phenomenon of business cycles and/or crises cannot exist.

In the end "the ultimate reason for all real crises always remains the poverty and restricted consumption of the masses, in the face of the drive of

[11]If the value of m_1 is 0.8, the economy moves on the upper cumulative disequilibrium path. On the contrary, if its value is 1.9, the economy runs into the depression.

capitalist production to develop the productive forces as if only the absolute consumption capacity of society set a limit to them."[12]

3.1.3 Mathematical Appendix

Rising realwage rate–Falling rate of profit type model

(Notation)
ω: correspondence coefficient of labour market
e^*: critical rate of unemployment
ν: growth rate of labour supply

(Model)
Production technique:

$$X_t = \sigma K_t, \qquad \sigma : const. \tag{3.18}$$

$$N_t = n X_t, \qquad n : const. \tag{3.19}$$

Equilibrium:

$$X_t = R_t N_t + I_t \tag{3.20}$$

Profit rate:

$$r_t = \frac{X_t - R_t N_t}{K_t} \tag{3.21}$$

Accumulation:

$$K_{t+1} = K_t + I_t \tag{3.22}$$

Bargaining equation:

$$\frac{R_t - R_{t-1}}{R_{t-1}} = \omega\left(\frac{N_t}{L_t} - e^*\right) \tag{3.23}$$

where ω and e^* are constants.
Labour supply:

$$L_{t+1} = (1 + \nu) L_t, \qquad \nu : const. \tag{3.24}$$

[12]K.Marx, *Capital*, vol. III, p.615.

Variables: X, K, N, R, I, r, L
Parameters: $\sigma, n, \omega, e^*, \nu$

(Reduced form of the model)
If we denote the rate of employment as e_t, from Eq.(3.18), (3.19) and (3.24),

$$e_{t+1} = \frac{N_{t+1}}{L_{t+1}} \tag{3.25}$$
$$= \frac{n\sigma K_{t+1}}{(1+\nu)L_t}. \tag{3.26}$$

On the other hand, from Eq.(3.18),(3.19),(3.20) and (3.22),

$$K_{t+1} = K_t + X_t - R_t N_t \tag{3.27}$$
$$= \frac{1+\sigma(1-nR_t)}{\sigma n} N_t. \tag{3.28}$$

Then the reduced form can be expressed as:

$$e_{t+1} = \frac{(1+\sigma(1-nR_t))e_t}{1+\nu} \tag{3.29}$$

$$R_{t+1} = \{1+\omega(e_{t+1}-e^*)\}R_t. \tag{3.30}$$

(Brief explanation of the model)
The equilibrium value of rate of employment and the realwage rate is:

$$e_t = e^* \tag{3.31}$$

$$R_t = \frac{\sigma-\nu}{\sigma n}. \tag{3.32}$$

Rising productivity of labour–Falling the consumption demand type model

(Notation)
τ: labour productivity
μ: growth rate of labour productivity

(Model)
Production technique:

$$X_t = \sigma\delta_t K_t, \qquad \sigma : const. \tag{3.33}$$

$$N_t = n_t X_t \tag{3.34}$$

Equilibrium:

$$X_t = R_t N_t + I_t \tag{3.35}$$

Rate of accumulation:

$$g_t = \frac{I_t}{K_t} \tag{3.36}$$

Capital accumulation:

$$K_{t+1} = K_t + I_t \tag{3.37}$$

Real wage rate:

$$R_t = R_0, \qquad R_0 : const. \tag{3.38}$$

Investment function:

$$g_{t+1} = g_t + \beta(\delta_t - 1), \qquad \beta > 0 : const. \tag{3.39}$$

Labour productivity:

$$\tau_t = \frac{1}{n_t} \tag{3.40}$$

Growth rate of τ:

$$\tau_{t+1} = (1 + \mu)\tau_t, \qquad \mu > 0 : const. \tag{3.41}$$

Variables: $X, K, N, R, I, \delta, n, g, \tau$
Parameters: σ, β, μ

(Reduced form of the model)
From Eq.(3.33), (3.34), (3.36), (3.38) and (3.40), we obtain

$$\delta_t = \frac{g_t}{(1 - \frac{R_0}{\tau_t})\sigma}. \tag{3.42}$$

Substituting this into Eq.(3.39),

$$g_{t+1} = g_t + \beta(\frac{g_t}{(1 - \frac{R_0}{\tau_t})\sigma} - 1). \tag{3.43}$$

The system which is consisted of Eq.(3.41) and (3.43) suffices to determine the behavior of the rate of accumulation and the labour productivity.

(Brief explanation of the model)
The following equation must be satisfied so that the capital equipment can be utilized normally.

$$g_t = \sigma(1 - \frac{R_0}{\tau_t}). \tag{3.44}$$

Falling realwage rate–Falling the consumption demand type model

(Notation)
r_t^*: the desired rate of profit of capitalists

(Model)
Production technique:

$$X_t = \delta_t \sigma K_t, \qquad \sigma : \text{const.} \tag{3.45}$$

$$N_t = n X_t, \qquad n : \text{const.} \tag{3.46}$$

Equilibrium:

$$X_t = R_t N_t + I_t \tag{3.47}$$

The function of desired rate of profit:

$$r_t^* = m_1 g_{t-1} + m_0, \qquad m_1 > 0 \tag{3.48}$$

Mark-up pricing:

$$r_t^* = \sigma(1 - nR_t) \tag{3.49}$$

Capital accumulation:

$$K_{t+1} = K_t + I_t \tag{3.50}$$

Rate of accumulation:

$$g_t = \frac{I_t}{K_t} \tag{3.51}$$

Investment function:

$$g_{t+1} = g_t + \beta(\delta_t - 1), \qquad \beta > 0 : const. \tag{3.52}$$

Variables: $X, K, N, R, I, \delta, g, r^*$
Parameters: $\sigma, n, \beta, m_0, m_1$

(Reduced form of the model)
From Eq.(3.45),(3.46),(3.47),(3.51) and (3.52), we obtain,

$$g_{t+1} = g_t + \beta \left\{ \frac{g_t}{(1 - nR_t)\sigma} - 1 \right\}. \tag{3.53}$$

On the other hand, from Eq.(3.48) and (3.49),

$$R_{t+1} = \frac{1}{n}\left\{1 - \frac{1}{\sigma}(m_1 g_t + m_0)\right\}. \tag{3.54}$$

The system which is consisted of these two equations suffices to determine the behavior of g_t and R_t.

(Brief explanation of the model)
The capital equipment can be utilized normally, if the equation: $g_t = \sigma(1 - nR_t)$ is satisfied. This can be rewritten as:

$$g^* = m_1 g^* + m_0. \tag{3.55}$$

If the price is set by

$$R^* = \frac{1}{n}(1 - \frac{g^*}{\sigma}), \tag{3.56}$$

then the desired rate of profit of capitalists is realized.

3.1.4 Programs

```
10 '*********************************
20 ' Rising Real Wage Rate -
30 ' Falling Rate of Profit type Model
40 '*********************************
50 PERIOD=60
60 DIM R(PERIOD),G(PERIOD),E(PERIOD)
70 '
80 '****** Parameters *******
90 SIG=.25
100 NC=4
110 NU=.05
120 OMEGA=.3
130 ES=.7
140 '
150 '****** Equilibrium *******
160 GS=NU
170 RS=(SIG - NU)/NC/SIG
180 '
190 '******* Initial Condition *******
200 T=0
210 R(0)=.16
220 E(0)=.7
230 G(0)=SIG * (1 - NC * R(0))
240 '
250 '******* Computation *******
260 PRINT "time     e "; "R     g"
270 FOR T=1 TO PERIOD
280 E(T)=(1+SIG * (1 - NC * R(T - 1))) * E(T - 1)/(1+NU)
290 R(T)=(1+OMEGA * (E(T) - ES)) * R(T - 1)
300 G(T)=SIG * (1 - NC * R(T))
310 PRINT T,E(T),R(T),G(T)
320 NEXT T
330 END
```

```
10 '*****************************************
20 ' Rising Productivity of Labour -
30 ' Falling the Consumption Demand type Model
40 '*****************************************
50 PERIOD=50
60 DIM G(PERIOD),TAU(PERIOD),DEL(PERIOD)
70 '
80 '******* Parameters *******
90 SIG=.25
100 BETA=.01
110 MU=.02
120 R0=.25
130 '
140 '******* Initial Condition *******
150 T=0
160 TAU(0)=.35
170 G(0)=.1
180 DEL(0)=G(0)/(1 - R0/TAU(0))/SIG
190 '
200 '******* Computation *******
210 PRINT " time      g      "; "X/N      del"
220 FOR T=1 TO PERIOD
230 G(T)=G(T - 1)+BETA * (DEL(T - 1) - 1)
240 TAU(T)=(1+MU) * TAU(T - 1)
250 DEL(T)=G(T)/(1 - R0/TAU(T))/SIG
260 PRINT T,G(T),TAU(T),DEL(T)
270 NEXT T
280 END
```

```
10 '*****************************************
20 ' Falling Real Wage Rate -
30 ' Falling the Consumption Demand type Model
40 '*****************************************
50 PERIOD=10
60 DIM G(PERIOD),R(PERIOD),DEL(PERIOD)
70 '
80 '******* Parameters *******
90 SIG=.25
100 NC=4
110 M0= - 0.05
120 M1=0.8
130 '
140 '******* Initial Condition *******
150 T=0
160 G(0)=.12
170 R(0)=.2
180 DEL(0)=G(0)/(1 - NC * R(0))/SIG
190 '
200 '******* Computation *******
210 PRINT " time      g      "; "r      del"
220 FOR T=1 TO PERIOD
230 R(T)=(1 - (M0+M1 * G(T - 1))/SIG/NC
240 G(T)=G(T - 1)+BETA * (DEL(T - 1) - 1)
250 DEL(T)=G(T)/(1 - NC * R(T))/SIG
260 PRINT T,G(T),R(T),DEL(T)
270 NEXT T
280 END
```

3.2 Theories of Business Cycles

In this section, we classify and examine two types of business cycle theories of orthodox economics. The first type, including Schumpeter's and Hayek's, focus attention on the role of technical change. They conclude that business cycles will occur even if effective demand does not play an important role in changing the income level. In other words, in their business cycle models, full employment is assured throughout the whole cycle. The differences between Schumpeter's and Hayek's theories is brought about by the different ways they approach the issue of technical change that is central in both theories. Schumpeter investigates the effect of the introduction of new techniques, or innovations, whereas Hayek treats technical change as a movement toward a more advantageous method within the existing technique. Schumpeter and Hayek are similar in character, in that they both made light of, if not neglected, the demand side factors.

The second type of theory, which includes those of Hicks, Samuelson, Kalecki, Kaldor and Harrod, considers the business cycle to be caused by demand side factors. They are all based upon Keynes's principle of effective demand, or multiplier theory, which regards investment demand as determining the level of income. Because Keynes's theory views investment only as a component of effective demand, they attempt to go beyond Keynes, by taking into account such subjects as the interaction between income and investment, the increase of productive capacity by investment, and the relation between the increased capacity and effective demand. They vary according to the different investment functions they assume.

3.2.1 Schumpeter

The essence of what Schumpeter said about the business cycle is that the introduction of technical progress in a capitalist economy is sufficient to bring about business cycle. In other words, in a capitalist economy, an economic wave is caused when technical progress takes place, and this wave is to be recognized as the business cycle.[13] Schumpeter's business cycle

[13]The most refined form of Schumupeter's business cycle theory is to be found in his *Business Cycles*.

model in its simplest form, which he called the pure model, proceeds through a series of phases described below.[14]

Schumpeter's business cycle model starts from a state of stationary flow, where Walrasian equilibrium reproduces itself at constant rates as time proceeds. All of the net product is consumed. The appearance of unknown new techniques, or innovation, forces the economy to depart from equilibrium, and boom, or what Schumpeter called "prosperity", begins. The investment of the first entrepreneur which embodies the innovation, starts as only a narrow investment stream, but as the rest of the firms follow him, innovation spreads quickly over the whole economic system.

The entrepreneur who first introduces innovation has to deal with an unfamiliar business. He, who takes the lead, must be gifted with ambition as well as the objective circumstances for carrying out the innovation. Through his experience, some of the difficulties with the new techniques will be eliminated, enabling increasing numbers of other entrepreneurs with less ambition and poorer circumstances to follow the path of innovation.

As there was no unemployment in the old equilibrium, workers who were working for firms using old techniques must be transferred to firms using new techniques, in order to utilize the equipment which embodies the new techniques. The fund necessary both for employing the workers and for creating new equipment is financed through credit creation by the banks. Using this fund, the entrepreneur bids for factors of production, which leads to an increase in effective demand and a rise in prices. The total output of the economy increases accordingly as the productivity of the new techniques exceeds that of the old one. In the boom, net investment occurs, and profit appears.

When innovation has spread throughout the whole system, investment decreases, and recession begins, leading to a new equilibrium. During recession, the decrease in investment demand is compensated for by the increase in consumption demand. Recession should be recognized as a time of harvesting, when the larger production achieved by innovation is distributed to the consumers.

Throughout the whole cycle, a deficiency of effective demand never develops, and full employment is assured. During the boom, rapid increases in investment demand caused by innovation generates disequilibrium. But

[14] J.A.Schumpeter, *Business Cycles*, p.130.

this disequilibrium is in the nature of excess demand, as mentioned before. During recession, the increase in consumption demand compensates for the decrease in investment demand. This is due to an actual tendency to move towards a state of equilibrium.

Schumpeter's first and most important contribution to business cycle theory lies in the fact that he pointed out the importance of technical progress as one of the major inducements of investment in the capitalist economy. His second contribution consists in working out the mechanism of a cumulative increase of investment during booms caused by the competition among firms rushing to adopt the new techniques. Thus, he could account for some of the significant features of the boom, such as the restriction of consumption caused by the growth of investment.

His limit consists in not realising that the downward phase of the cycle, or his recession, is a downward cumulative process of disequilibrium. The decrease in investment at the end of the boom cannot be compensated by the increase in consumption as Schumpeter assumed. Because, when investment decreases and the profit rate falls, capitalists are not willing to maintain the high level of production that ensures full employment. Thus, the end of innovation and also of boom, brings about a shortage of effective demand, leading to a downward cumulative process of disequilibrium.

Let us build a simple model of Schumpeter's business cycle theory. There are two sectors in the economy, an old sector and a new sector which produce the same products by old techniques and new techniques. Let $X1$, $X2$ and X denote the real output of the old sector, the output of the new sector, and total real output respectively,

$$X_t = X1_t + X2_t. \tag{3.57}$$

Products can be used as both production and consumption goods. Factors of production are production goods and direct labour. Production goods are fixed equipments with unlimited durability. Suppose v_1 units of fixed equipments and n_1 units of labour are required to produce one unit of product in the old sector and v_2 units of fixed equipments and n_2 units of labour are required to produce one unit of product in the new sector. We assume

$$v_1 \geq v_2, \qquad n_1 > n_2$$

so that, new techniques are have an advantage over old techniques regardless of the level of real wage rate.

Let $N1$ and $K1$ denote the amount of labour and fixed equipments used in the old sector. $N2$ and $K2$ are similar factors used in the new sector. The level of production of the old sector, $X1$, is determined by the minimum of $K1/v_1$ and $N1/n_1$. The output of the new sector is determined by the minimum of $K2/v_2$ and $N2/n_2$.

Investment demand of each sector is determined as follows. As regards the old sector, there is no investment throughout the cycle. In the old equilibrium, as labour is fully employed, further investment does not make sense. After the new techniques have been introduced, capitalists in the old sector are too threatened by the appearance of the new techniques that they will not invest in the old technology, no matter how profitable the investment might be in the short run. I_t is probable that some of the capitalists in the old sector invest in the new techniques. In this model, we shall include such investment in the investment function of the new sector.

The extent to which difficulties involved in implementing the new techniques have been eliminated, and the level of confidence of the imitators in the practicality of the new techniques, can be measured by the past results of production in the new sector. Therefore, we shall assume that investment in the new sector is in direct proportion to the amount of production in the new sector in the previous period. Thus, we get investment function of the new sector:

$$I_t = \gamma X2_{t-1}. \tag{3.58}$$

As there is no depreciation, we have:

$$K2_{t+1} = K2_t + I_t. \tag{3.59}$$

By subtracting investment from total production X, we get consumption demand C:

$$X_t = C_t + I_t. \tag{3.60}$$

It is assumed that there is sufficient effective demand for products to assure full employment throughout the cycle.
The constant labour supply, L, is fully employed in either sector, as there is no want of effective demand:

$$L = N1_t + N2_t. \tag{3.61}$$

The business cycle proceeds through the following phases:
The old equilibrium:
As new techniques have not come into existence:

$$X2 = N2 = K2 = I = 0. \tag{3.62}$$

Suppose that a sufficient amount of $K1$ held by the old sector, so that labour supply, L, is employed by the old sector alone:

$$N1_t = L. \tag{3.63}$$

All of the products from the old sector, or the total output, to be consumed is given by:

$$Xt = X1_t = \frac{N1_t}{n_1} \tag{3.64}$$

$$X_t = C_t. \tag{3.65}$$

The boom:
The boom is essentially a phase of accumulation opened by appearance of someone who "takes the lead". We assume that the new sector has the financial ability to employ the necessary labour, $N2$, to utilize its fixed equipments, $K2$:

$$N2_t = \frac{n_2}{v_2} K2_t \tag{3.66}$$

$$X2_t = \frac{N2_t}{n_2}. \tag{3.67}$$

Employment in the old sector, N1, is determined by subtracting the new sector employment, $N2$, from the total labour supply, L:

$$N1_t = L - N2_t. \tag{3.68}$$

And the production of the old sector is:

$$X1_t = \frac{N1_t}{n_1}. \tag{3.69}$$

Figure 3.4 Production in the old sector and new sector

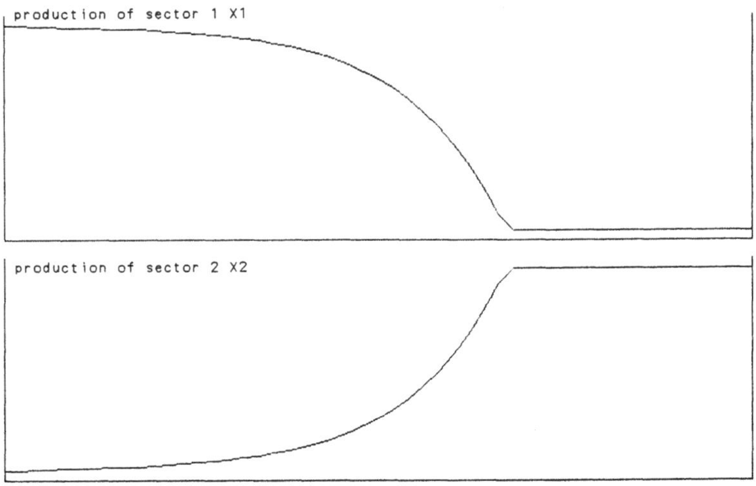

Let the time of the old equilibrium be the period 0. The investment by the entrepreneur, who takes the lead, takes place in the first period, which makes boom start:

$$I_1 = \bar{I}, \qquad \bar{I} > 0. \tag{3.70}$$

Thereafter, occurs the phase, in which continuing investment in the new sector increases the amount of production equipment, and this increase in equipment leads to an increase in output, which in turn increases investment.

In the first period, although investment has begun in the new sector, there is no input of labour to, or output of products from that sector. The old sector produces the same amount as in the old equilibrium, which is the total production. Consumption falls below the old equilibrium level by the same amount as the output used for the new sector accumulation. After the second period, the new sector begins to produce goods. A transfer of labour from the old sector to the new sector takes place. As the products of the new sector appear on the market, total output increases. With the increase in production of the new sector, investment demand expands.

If there exists sufficient quantities of labour supply, transfer of labour from the old equilibrium continues and boom goes on. In the old sector, a decrease in employment equivalent to the increased employment in the new sector takes place. Along with employment, $N1$, production, $X1$, decreases in the old sector. After a considerable time has passed, $K2$, $X2$, $N2$ and I rise gradually. With increased investment, profits also increase. The ratio of consumption to production, C/X, falls, and the ratio of investment to production, I/X, rises. Whether the consumption level, C, increases or decreases depends on the particular conditions.

Recession and the New Equilibrium:

Recession is a phase in which the economy proceeds to a new equilibrium. During recession, the fruit of innovation is distributed to the consumers. When the transfer of labour has been completed, the boom ends. Let us assume that the labour demanded by the new sector, $N2$, exceeds the labour supply, L, in the period s. Capitalists will not invest in the period s or thereafter:

$$I(t) = 0, \qquad t = s, s+1, ...$$

In this model, consumption demand rises instantaneously and compensates for the decrease in investment demand. Recession is an instantaneous process leading directly to the new equilibrium.

3.2.2 Hayek

Hayek, like Schumpeter, considers technical change to be an important factor in the business cycle. For Hayek, technical change means technical substitution within the existing technical knowledge, as distinct from Schumpeter's innovation. An outline of his business cycle theory is as follows:

In the early years of his career, Hayek believed that technical substitution was caused by monetary factors such as changes in interest rates.[15] But later, he viewed real wages as the cause of technical substitution.[16] When real wages falls, a production method which utilizes more labour relative to production goods will be chosen as a more advantageous method. On the contrary, when real wages rise, a more labour saving production method will be chosen. Hayek called this type of technical change, caused by fluctuations in real wages, the "Ricardo Effect".

Hayek also assumes that full employment, or equilibrium, is assured throughout the cycle. This assumption is open to criticism. Since, though Hayek was quite clear on this point in his early works, he did not discuss on this assumption in his later works.[17] But, his theory can be understood most consistently on this assumption.

If a labour saving production method is chosen, which utilizes more production goods relative to labour, the demand for production goods increases. A larger portion of the labour supply will be utilized in the production goods sector to meet the increasing demand. The expansion of the production goods sector, under the assumption of full employment, means

[15] F.A.von Hayek, *Preise und Produktion.*

[16] F.A.von Hayek, *Profits, Interests and Investment*, pp.3-4.

[17] For his early works, see *Preise und Produktion.* For his later works, see *Profits, Interests and Investment.*

contraction of consumption goods sector. This state is recognized as the upward phase of business cycle. If a labour intensive production method is chosen, which utilizes more labour relative to production goods, the demand for production goods decreases, and an increased share of the labour supply will be employed in the consumption goods sector. The consumption goods sector expands and production goods sector contracts. This state is the downward phase of the cycle.

What makes the real wage rate fluctuate? Hayek did not express himself fully on this point. But if we supplement his theory using his characteristic ideas and viewpoints, we can close his model. Hayek reasoned that there was a time lag, or production period, between input and output. Therefore, the amount of consumption goods produced at any given point in time depends on the amount of labour input in the consumption goods sector at a point in time preceding the current production period. In other words, it depends on whether or not the consumption goods sector was expanding at that past point in time. As the equivalence of demand and supply for consumption goods is assured by disregarding problems concerning effective demand, total consumption demand is determined by the amount of consumption goods produced.

If the consumption demand of capitalists does not fluctuate sharply, the consumption demand of workers must fluctuate along with the production of consumption goods. To simplify, we assume that laborers do not save. Then, the level of real wage rate, which is determined by the amount of consumption goods consumed by the laborers and the fixed level of employment, will consequently depend on the level of consumption goods production. Thus, the level of the real wage rate is determined by the phase of the business cycle that was prevailing in the period preceding the production period.

From the above assumptions, the business cycle is derived. In the upward phase of the cycle, the real wage rate rises and a labour saving method of production is chosen. The production goods sector expands and the consumption goods sector contracts during this phase. After the production period has passed, there comes a time when the production of consumer goods decreases and the real wage rate falls. When real wage rate falls, a change to a labour intensive method of production takes place, and the consumption goods sector expands. This is the downward phase of the business cycle.

The expansion of the consumption goods sector, after the production period, will raise the real wage rate and bring about the upward phase of business cycle. In this way, upward and downward phases of the business cycle alternate. Hayek's theory can be refined if we take into account possible changes in the length of the time lag or production period, but this would not alter the main aspects of the model.[18]

Hayek's model made a contribution to business cycle theory by inquiring deeply into two technical aspects of production. First, he took into account the possibility of technical change, or technical substitution, caused by changes in the real wage rate, even if technical knowledge has not altered. Technical substitution is an inevitable feature which derives from the central role of profit-seeking behavior in capitalist society. Second, he examined explicitly the necessity of a time lag, or production period, between input and output. In this way, he drew attention to the fact that amount of output at a given point in time is restricted by the input of factors of production at a past time. Hayek's thoughts on these two aspects are reasonable, and contain insights that business cycle theory should attend to.

However, Hayek's theory is insufficient because it assumes full employment. This insufficiency reveals itself most in the following sequence: During empirically observed business cycles, it is usual that both the production goods sector and the consumption goods sector expand in the upward phases of the cycle. And, in downward phases, both sectors normally contract. In Hayek's theory, the expansion of one sectors always lead to the contraction of the other. What causes this phenomenon?

To make this point clear, let us consider how investment demand is determined and what happens to the size of the production goods sector, when the real wage rate rises. According to Hayek, when the real wage rate rises, the consumption goods sector must contract and the production goods sector expand. Expansion of the production goods sector means an increase in investment. It is true that a rise in the real wage rate reduces the profit rate of the consumption goods sector and contracts it. If technical substitution toward a labour saving production method takes place, as

[18] Y.Aiba, "Production Period and Business Cycle - A Hayekian Business Cycle Model -" (in Japanese), *The Bulletin of Nihon Fukusi University*, No.74-2, Dec. 1987, Japan.

Hayek assumed it would, there will be a further reduction of employment in the consumption goods sector. As a rise in the real wage rate reduces the profit rates in both sectors, total investment demand from both sectors must decline. A fall in investment demand reduces production goods prices and the profit rate in the production goods sector. The output of the production goods sector will fall and the production goods sector will contract. Thus, if we assume a probable change of investment demand, it is likely that a simultaneous contraction of both sectors will take place.

But, in Hayek's model, a contraction of the production goods sector always leads to an expansion of the consumption goods sector. This is because of the assumption of full employment combined with the lack of an investment function. It is two different things to decide which technical method should be adopted for the future production and to determine the amount of production goods that should be demanded for future production. In his business cycle theory, Hayek gives an account of the former but not of the latter. That means his model is lacking an of investment function in the true sense of the term. Instead, he introduces an assumption of full employment, which assures what is produced in the production goods industries, by whatever technical method, finds a demand for itself. So, it is the full employment assumption that brings about peculiar behavior of investment demand in his theory.

3.2.3 Samuelson, Hicks and Frisch

The Samuelson-Hicks type model

All of the theories discussed so far in this chapter assume the full employment of labour and thus abstract away from the problem of the "realization of commodities". In contrast, the theories which are analyzed here center upon the realization problem. *The Samuelson-Hicks type model* postulates that economic fluctuations are the result of an interaction between the phenomena described by the multiplier theory and the acceleration principle. Before explaining the Samuelson-Hicks model, we summarise the multiplier theory of Keynes.

To simplify the discussion, we assume a closed economy which consists of private sectors only. The demand for the products which have been produced in a certain period and have the value X consists of the replacement demand, D, consumption demand, C, and investment demand, I. The equilibrium condition of the product market is expressed as:

$$X = D + C + I.$$

If we subtract the products needed for replacement from the aggregate product, we get a net product which is equal to the national income: $Y(\equiv X - D)$. The equation can be rewritten as:

$$Y = C + I.$$

On the other hand, since Keynes defines the residual $(Y - C)$ as saving, S, the equilibrium condition can be shown as:

$$S = I.$$

If we suppose that saving is a constant proportion of income $(S = sY)$, we get:

$$sY = I \quad or \quad Y = I/s.$$

That is, given a certain level of investment, the level of income (production) is determined so as to equalize supply and demand. Accordingly, we can say that the change in income is equal to the product of the saving rate and the change in investment:

$$\text{change in } Y - \text{change in } I/s.$$

The multiplier theory connects I and Y in such a way to give the relationship: investment $\Rightarrow$ income. Further, the increment of income generated exceeds the increment of investment, since the propensity to save is less than unity. This is "the Multiplier Effect".

In Keynes's theory, investment was treated simply as a component of aggregate demand which determines the level of national income. The urgent problem for Keynes was how to decrease idle capacity and mass unemployment. An analysis of the relationship between production capacity and effective demand was not his main concern. After Keynes, many economists tried to dynamize his theory and/or combine the multiplier theory and the acceleration principle so as to explain the occurrence of economic fluctuations. Samuelson's dynamic model[19] and Hicks' trade cycle theory[20] are the most important work among them.

One of the characteristics of Hicks' theory is that it assumed an explosive system and the cycle is explained by the existence of a ceiling (full-employment, *etc.*) and a floor (where gross investment= 0) between which the system oscillates. In this sense, the theory of Hicks is sometimes referred to as "the constrained cycle or billiards model". If the acceleration principle is applied to the downward phase of cycle, the net investment becomes negative. But since the absolute value of negative net investment cannot exceed the depreciation of capital, there exists a lower limit on negative net investment. Taking this into account, Hicks built a nonlinearity into the acceleration principle, which is the second important characteristic of his theory. Thirdly, Hicks introduced the idea of independent investment which grows at a constant rate in order to depict an economy that grows cyclically.

We have constructed a model which possesses the above characteristics. However, let us first discuss a system which is not constrained. Leaving aside, for simplicity, both the government and foreign trade sector, we consider an economy which consists only of private sectors. Investment demand consists of a part which is induced by the increase in income, and a part which is independent from the change of income and public investment.[21] The first two are induced investment, I_t, and the latter is independent investment, B_t. The equilibrium condition for production is:

[19] P.A.Samuelson, "Interactions Between the Multiplier Analysis and the Principle of Acceleration," *Review of Economic Statistics*, 1939.

[20] J.R.Hicks, *A Contribution to Theory of the Trade cycle*, 1950.

[21] "Public investment is that ...which occurs in direct response to inventions, and much of the 'long-range' investment (as Harrod calls it) which is only expected to pay for itself over a long period. "(Hicks, *op. cit.*, p.59).

$$Y_t = C_t + I_t + B_t. \tag{3.71}$$

We introduce a time-lag in both consumption and induced investment. That is, we suppose that consumption demand depends on income in the previous period, and that induced investment is proportional to the increased increment of income in the previous period; $(Y_{t-1} - Y_{t-2})$. Next, although independent investment is supposed to be determined by various factors, it grows at a constant rate, G_b, which is given exogenously. Above equation can be rewritten as a second order difference equation:

$$Y_t - (c + \gamma)Y_{t-1} + \gamma Y_{t-2} - B_0(1 + G_b)^t = 0. \tag{3.72}$$

If the structural parameters such as the marginal propensity to consume, the coefficient of investment, *etc.* are stable, then the all of national income can be calculated from this equation sequentially. For instance, if c= 0.8, $\gamma = 2.5$, $G_b = 0.03$, $B_0 = 1$, Y_{-1}= 2 and Y_{-2}= 1, then:

$$\begin{aligned} Y_0 &= (0.8 + 2.5)Y_{-1} - 2.5Y_{-2} + 1 = 5.1, \\ Y_1 &= (0.8 + 2.5)Y_0 - 2.5Y_{-1} + 1 = 12.86. \end{aligned}$$

In such a way, we can calculate values for Y_2, Y_3, ..., and determine the movement of Y_t.

Generally speaking, if the coefficient of investment exceeds unity, the system becomes explosive, and conversely if it is less than unity, the system becomes convergent. Whether the cyclical movements occur within the non-constrained system or not depends on both the value of the marginal propensity to consume and the coefficient of investment. With a given coefficient of investment, the smaller the marginal propensity to consume becomes, the greater the possibility of cyclical movement.

Assume that the marginal propensity to consume is 0.8 and the coefficient of investment is 2.5. Under these conditions, the system is explosive. Whether the system diverges upwards or downwards from equilibrium depends on the initial income conditions. For example, assume that until the period 0 the economy moved along the dynamic equilibrium path and in the first period an external shock (e.g. a temporary increase of independent investment) occurred. Then the economy diverges from the equilibrium path upwards and from that point onwards there is a continuing process of cumulative disequilibrium.[22]

To simplify the discussion, we would assume that the depreciation of capital is equal to zero and the acceleration principle does not function after income begins to decrease.

The ceiling of full-employment, which determines the upper limit of the cycle, becomes higher when the productivity of labour increases and the labour supply increases. But, we also assume that the growth rate of productivity and that of labour supply are equal to zero. That is, the full employment income, Y_F, is a constant. Accordingly, the economy necessarily reaches the ceiling as it moves upwards. Suppose that the economy reaches the ceiling during the period t. The level of income shrinks, compared to what it would be without constrains, and Y_t has to take on the values of Y_F. At the same time, the realized investment falls below the previous level of investment, which lowers the level of income in the next period. If the income in the period $t+1$ still exceeds Y_F, the level of income will be forced down to Y_F, and investment will drop to zero because of the acceleration principle. When this occurs, income decreases drastically and falls below the full-employment income, Y_F.

If income is less than the level of Y_F, the acceleration principle does not work and investment is equal to zero. The economy diverges downward from the equilibrium path. Once the economy begins to move to downward, it converges to the lower dynamic equilibrium income, Y_{Lt}, which grows at a constant rate, as long as no external shocks are given. When the system reaches the lower dynamic equilibrium income, Y_{Lt}, the acceleration principle begins to work again since Y_{Lt} grows at a constant rate, G_b.[23]

[22] This means that the solution satisfies the condition:

$$Y_0 - Y_0^* \geq 0, \qquad (Y_1 - Y_1^*) - \lambda(Y_0 - Y_0^*) > 0$$

where λ is the characteristic root and is greater than unity. If $\lambda > 1$, Y_t diverges from the equilibrium value Y_t^* once initial upper disequilibrium movement $(Y_0 - Y_0^*)$ start.

[23] Y_{Lt} is the particular solution of the difference equation:

$$Y_t - cY_{t-1} - B_0(1+G_b)^t = 0.$$

Investment is induced and income increases through the mechanism of the multiplier process. Then the economy moves back into the non-constrained region and continues upwards. The catalyst which makes the economy move upward is independent investment. If independent investment is held constant, the economy will remain in a state of lower equilibrium and does not upward.

An example of the cycle generated by this model is shown in Figure 3.5.

Figure 3.5 The movements of income and investment

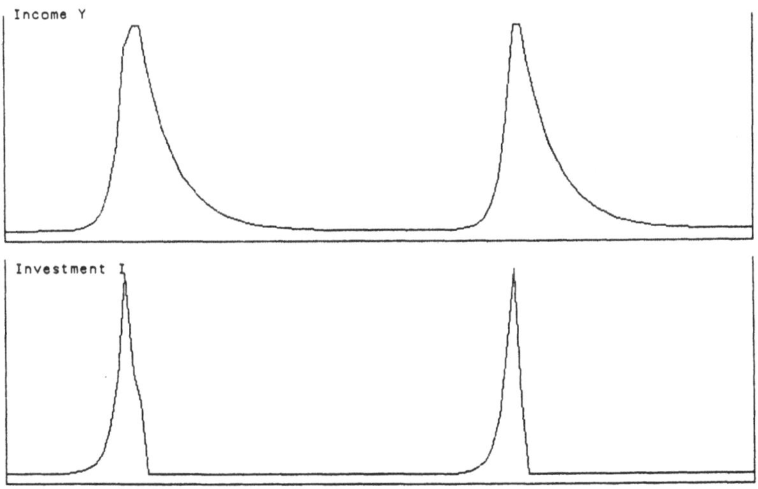

And the general solution is expressed as:

$$Y_t = (Y_0 - Y_{Lt})c^t + Y_{Lt}$$

where $Y_{Lt} = \dfrac{B_0}{1 - c/(1+G_b)^t}(1+G_b)^t$. As c is less than unity, Y_t converges to Y_{Lt}.

Hicks tried to explain the existence of the business cycle, by assuming that the economic system is unstable and that there exists upper and lower limits. In contrast to this idea, there exists the random shock theory which asserts that the economic system itself is stable, and that cyclical movements are generated by random shocks. Adherents of this theory include Frisch, Slutzky and Kalecki.[24]

The Hicks-Frisch type model

Here we call the model which introduces a random term in the Samuelson-Hicks model *the Hicks-Frisch type model.* This model economy is supposed to be stable without a random term and converges to the equilibrium path over time. We assume that the economy moves on the equilibrium path until the 0-th period and random shocks, $u_1, u_2, \ldots$, are given after the first period. Then, we can demonstrate, by simulation, that almost regular cyclical movements are produced in this model if the sequence of random shocks, u_t, have a Normal Distribution. (See Figure 3.6)

Figure 3.6 An example (Hicks-Frisch type)

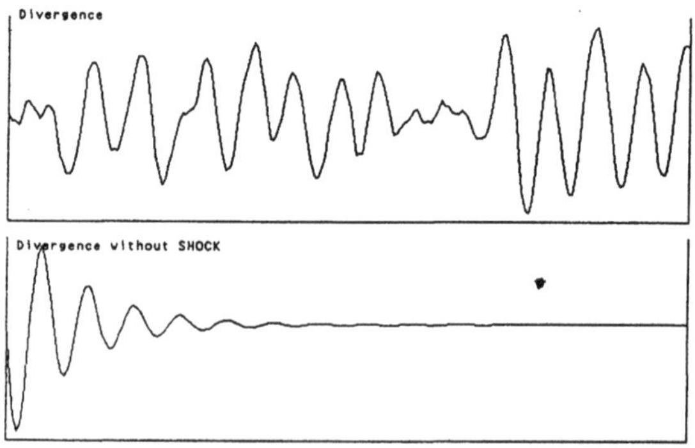

[24]R.Frisch, "Propagation Problems And Impulse Problems in Dynamic Economics," in *Economic Essays in Honor of Gustav Cassel*, 1933.
E.Slutzky, "Summation of Random Causes as the Source of Cycle Process," *Econometrica*, 1935.
M.Kalecki, "A Macrodynamic Theory of Business Cycle," *Econometrica*, 1935.

In this theory, the fluctuation of income is generated by interrelations between the autonomous mechanisms of the system itself and the random shocks. If the solution of the system without random shocks is damped oscillatory, the larger the part of fluctuation which is explained by the autonomous mechanism the smaller the extent of damping. But as the extent becomes larger the part of fluctuation which can be explained by random shocks becomes larger. In addition, if the solution of the system is damped monotonically, the fluctuation of this model can be completely explained by random shocks. In this sense, as the extent of damping becomes large, the cycle generated is attributed to the random shocks. That is, the reason why the cyclical movements are generated seems to be open.

Some have criticised the acceleration principle on the ground that t assumes the full utilization of capital equipment and it ignores the problem of funds. As long as the Samuelson-Hicks type model purports to explain the business cycle through the interaction between the multiplier and the acceleration principle, it cannot avoid such criticism.

Investment is a component of the aggregate demand for products and at the same time it becomes a part of productive capacity when it is introduced in the productive process ("duality of investment"). Nevertheless, the Samuelson-Hicks model neglects the latter effect. This is a important theoretical fault.

Hicks says in his *Trade Cycle* that "[t]he first of these points, which we have to attribute to Mr.Harrod, is of course his insistence on the propriety, indeed the necessity, of approaching the business cycle as a problem of an expanding economy. What we have to study, he emphasizes, is not fluctuation as such, but fluctuation about a rising trend".[25] So, he conducts his analysis on the assumption that the economic system is explosive. To the extent that Hicks' theory is founded on the idea of an inherent instability in the capitalist economy, we believe it has some merit. However, in the theory the upper turning point is explained by the "exogenous" factor of full employment, the determinant of the dynamic equilibrium path is independent investment which grows at a constant rate, and the lower turning point is explained by the autonomous increase of independent investment. To explain the turning points of the business cycle as due to exogenous factors seems to be a grave theoretical fault in any dynamic theory of a

[25]Hicks J.R., *op. cit.*, pp.7-8.

capitalist economy. For the same reason, we find the random shock theory to be an inadequate theoretical structure.

3.2.4 Kalecki and Kaldor

The following business cycle model of *the Kalecki-Kaldor type* is found in Kalecki's excellent paper [26] and Kaldor's study.[27] It attempts to analyse the cycle by combining multiplier theory with the so-called "Profit Principle". First, the equilibrium condition of the commodity market is:

$$sY_t - A = I_t \tag{3.73}$$

where s is the marginal propensity to save, and A denotes the basic consumption and is assumed to be positive constant. According to the Profit Principle, investment is supposed to be determined by the rate of profit. The rate of profit is defined as profits/capital. If income distribution is unchanged, profits are determined by the level of income. So we can specify an investment function based on the Profit Principle as:

$$I_t = aY_{t-1} - bK_t + B, 0 < a, 0 < b, 0 < B(const.) \tag{3.74}$$

where B denotes autonomous investment.

If we start with the assumption that the quantity of capital equipment is constant, then as the level of income increases (decreases), the rate of profit rises (falls) and therefore investment increases (decreases). If net investment is positive, capital equipment is increasing and this will have a negative effect on the rate of profit. Hence, investment will decrease as capital equipment increases. Conversely, if gross investment is below depreciation (that is, net investment is negative), investment will increase.

As long as usable the capital equipment is not scrapped, the absolute value of negative net investment cannot exceed the depreciation rate. As can be easily observed, the investment function specified above does not

[26] "A Macrodynamic Theory of the Business Cycle," *Econometrica*, 1935. *The Theory of Economic Dynamics*, 1954.

[27] "A Model of the Trade Cycle," *Economic Journal*, 1940.

work when $I_t \leq -dK_t$. Instead of this, the investment is determined by

$$I_t = -dK_t \tag{3.75}$$

where d: the rate of depreciation, const. The stock of capital equipment changes according to:

$$K_{t+1} = K_t + I_t. \tag{3.76}$$

What has been stated suffices to construct a model of the Kalecki-Kaldor type. For example, if we specify the values of the parameters as: $s = 0.2, a = 0.3, b = 0.5, d = 0.05, A = 10$, and $B = 10$, then the model exhibits the regularly cyclical movements depicted in Figure 3.7.

Figure 3.7 An example (Kalecki-Kaldor type)

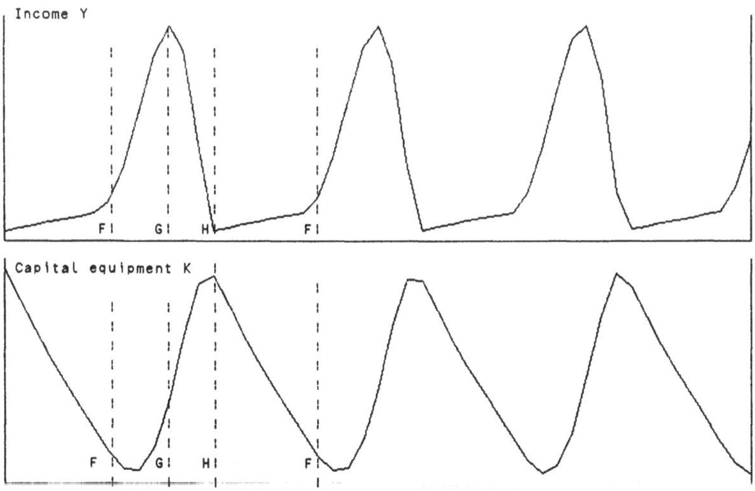

We now examine the regular cyclical movements of the economy according to this model. Assume the initial situation of the economy is as follows: net investment is equal to zero and the level of investment is such that the multiplier mechanism works (see point F in Figure 3.7). As income increases, investment also increases. The upward movement of cycles continues as the increasing investment generates increasing income. However, when gross investment exceeds depreciation, capital equipment increases and this has a negative effect on the self-stimulating relationship between investment and income. The greater the amount of capital equipment, the greater is the negative effect. Sooner or later, this negative effect cancels out the positive effect on income. At this point the increase in income and investment comes to a halt, and the period of prosperity is over (point G).

As investment is still positive at point G, the level of capital equipment increases further. The negative effect of an increase of capital works to decrease both investment and income. Income begins to decrease and this negatively influences investment. Investment decreases rapidly and ultimately turns negative and is below the rate of depreciation, *i.e.* $-dK_t$. Capital equipment now begins to decrease which has a positive effect on investment. After a while, the positive effect of this decrease in capital offsets the negative effect of the decrease of income, and the decrease of income and investment stop. The depression has now reached its fullest extent and the stage is set for the lower turning point of the cycle (point H).

As income begins to increase, investment also increases and the positive feedback mechanism moves the economy into the upward phase of the cycle (point F). The economy repeats the cyclical movement as examined above. Here we have explained the mechanism of one cycle, assuming that the economy which starts at point F comes back again to the same level of output at point H (closed trajectory).

In assessing the relative merits of this model the following points seem appropriate. First, a characteristic of this type of model is that investment is considered not only as a component of the aggregate demand, but also as potential productive equipment. In the Samuelson-Hicks model, if net investment is constant, the level of income will also be constant as long as independent investment does not fluctuate. That is, the level of income can be stationary even if there exists a positive net investment. But in the Kalecki-Kaldor model, if net investment is positive, the capital equipment, *i.e.*, the productive capacity increases. That has a negative effect on investment and decreases income.

Secondly, in contrast with the acceleration principle which assumes that the investment is proportional to the increment of income, the profit principle theorizes capitalists' independent behavior such that investment is determined by the rate of profit. It is important to include these aspects in any model that hopes to comprehend the dynamics of the capitalist economy. In this sense, the Kalecki-Kaldor type model seems superior to the Samuelson-Hicks.

As is shown in Figure 3.7, if the initial value is a point outside the closed orbit, the economy moves spirally toward it, but if it is given as a point inside the closed orbit, the economy diverges from that point spirally toward the closed orbit. In this way, regular cyclical movements are produced by the endogenous mechanism in Kalecki-Kaldor model which is in contrast with the Samuelson-Hicks model which relies on exogenous stimuli.

The point at issue concerning the profit principle is that it assumes that an increase in capital equipment "always" has a negative effect on investment. Even during a phase in which capital equipment increases, the capitalists do not necessarily decrease investment, especially if there exists demand which exceeds the productive capacity.

3.2.5 Harrod

Although Harrod has published many papers and books on business cycles and growth theory since the 1930s[28], his theory has been considered to be inconsistent, from the mathematical point of view, since he does not present it by means of a closed mathematical model. But Harrod's theory which centers the capitalists' private investment behavior is very informative when we analyse the dynamics of the capitalist economy. Here, we have constructed a Harrodian model of the business cycle and examine its merits and deficiencies.

First, We assume that the equilibrium condition of the commodity market is satisfied, that is:

[28] R.F.Harrod, *The Trade Cycle: An Essay*, 1936. *Towards a Dynamic Economics*, 1948.

$$sY_t = I_t. \tag{3.77}$$

Harrod's model is characterized by an investment function known of "the Harrod-Okishio type". It is specified as:

$$\frac{I_t}{K_t} = \frac{I_{t-1}}{K_{t-1}} + \beta(v^* - v_{t-1}), \qquad \beta > 0 \tag{3.78}$$

$$v_t = \frac{K_t}{Y_t}. \tag{3.79}$$

The capital coefficient when the capital equipment is utilized at normal level is denoted by v^*.[29]

First, the investment function assumes that capitalists determine investment according to whether the actual rate of utilization is higher/lower than the normal rate of utilization. The investment of period t, or the capital equipment which is purchased in the period t will be employed in the period $t+1$. So capitalists have to anticipate the level of demand, the rate of utilization and so on in the period $t+1$, and evaluate the adequacy of the existing capital stock for the needs of the next period and make their investment decisions accordingly. Hence, strictly speaking, v_{t-1} should be called the expected value of the capital coefficient. The specification of an investment function like the one above is based on the assumption that capitalists' expectations are static.

Second, it is not the absolute value of investment but the relative value compared to the existing capital (I/K) that is determined by the rate of utilization. Even if the rate of utilization is the same (e.g. 110%), the level

[29] If we formulate the investment function according to Harrod's own spirit, it can be as follows:

$$\dot{G} = F(C_r - C), F(0) = 0, F' > 0$$

G: the growth rate of income, C_r: normal-marginal coefficient of capital, C: actual-marginal coefficient of capital.

This formulation has some drawbacks.

1) It abstracts the investment behavior of capitalists.

2)The gap $(C_r - C)$ does not represent the correct index that the capital is either too much or too little.

of investment is greater in a case where the existing capital is 1000, than if it is 100.

Third, the investment function assumes that capitalists maintain the rate of accumulation when capital equipment is utilized normally. This means that capitalists maintain not "the absolute level" of investment but "the growth rate" of it under the circumstances where capital equipment is neither too plentiful nor too scarce. But, If we assume that capitalists maintain "the absolute level" of investment, under the conditions stated above, capitalists do not invest at all. Then, although capital equipment continues to be utilized normally, both income, Y_t, and capital equipment, K_t, remains constant. Consequently, the ratio, K_t/Y_t, remains constant and investment is zero. Which is to say, in this model, equilibrium growth could be impossible. But to construct a dynamic model of a capitalist economy, a potential equilibrium growth path must be exist in the model. This is why we assume that capitalists maintain "the growth rate" of investment. Such investment behavior generates "Harrodian Instability" in the economy which we will explain shortly.

Now at the beginning of period t there exists the capital equipment, K_t, as the result of the previous accumulation activities of the capitalists. From the relative capital coefficient of the previous period and the normal capital coefficient, v^*, the rate of accumulation and investment for the current period is determined. Given a certain level of investment demand, income is determined by the multiplier mechanism and the capital coefficient and other model values, of the period t, are also calculated.

If the actual capital coefficient is equal to v^* (*i.e.* the capital equipment is utilized normally), the rate of accumulation is the same as that of previous period and the capital equipment will be utilized normally in the next period. That is, both the equilibrium condition of commodity market and the normal utilization of capital are satisfied. This growth path is called "the warranted growth path" and on this path the growth rate of income, G, is equal to s/v^* which is the same as the warranted rate of growth, G_w, in the Harrodian sense.

But, since the actual growth rate, G, is determined as the composite result of the production decisions which many capitalists make privately and individually, it is not necessarily equal to the warranted rate of growth, G_w. Once the actual growth path diverges from the warranted growth path, it cannot return to the warranted growth path again but it diverges from it cumulatively (***Harrod's Instability Principle***). The reason why is as follows: If the actual capital coefficient is below v^* (*i.e.* over utilization of capital), capitalists raise the capital coefficient compared to that of the previous period. As easily can be seen from the relation between the capital coefficient and the rate of accumulation; $v_t = s/g_t$, the capital coefficient falls if the rate of accumulation is raised. This functions to raise the rate of accumulation further. So the actual growth path diverges from the warranted growth path cumulatively in an upward direction.

Conversely, if the actual capital coefficient exceeds v^* (*i.e.* under utilization of capital), the mechanism described above operates in the opposite direction, and the actual growth path diverges from the warranted growth path in a cumulative downward direction. Therefore, we conclude that the growth path, which continues to satisfy both the equilibrium condition of the commodity market and the condition of normal utilization of capital, is unstable.

Figure 3.8 Harrodian Instability Principle

But such cumulative movements cannot continue forever. There exists a ceiling which is prescribed by both the full employment of labour and technical progress ("the natural rate of growth (G_n)"according to Harrod), and there exists also a floor which is encountered when gross investment reaches zero or basic consumption that grows in the long run. If the economy reaches such a ceiling or floor, it cannot remain there for very long. As the warranted rate of growth, G_w, changes, the actual rate of growth, G, becomes less than G_w and the cumulative growth process is reversed.

Here we discuss a case where the upper turning point is constrained by the ceiling G_n. The actual rate of growth, G, can be larger than the natural rate of growth, G_n, while idle capacity exists. But when the economy reaches the ceiling, the growth rate is constrained by G_n and therefore G equals G_n. If the inequality $G_n < G_w$ holds, the actual rate of growth must satisfy the relation: $G = G_n < G_w$. Because of the workings of the Instability Principle, the economy enters the downward cumulative process. If the inequality $G_n > G_w$ holds, the actual rate of growth can exceed G_w; $G = G_n > G_w$. In this case, capitalists continue to accumulate after the economy reaches the full employment ceiling and then inflation commences, also, capitalists' profits increase. Since the saving rate from profits is high, the overall saving rate rises according to the change in income distribution. This raises the warranted rate of growth, G_w, and it now exceeds the natural rate of growth G_n; $G_n < G_w$. In the end the relation; $G = G_n < G_w$ holds and the economy turns down.

As discussed above, in the Harrodian cyclical model the cyclical movement is explained by both the Instability Principle (the relationship between the actual growth path and the warranted growth path) and the shifting of the warranted growth path itself.

Harrod's Instability Principle is distinct, from the other orthodox models considered in this chapter, in the sense that it considers the important characteristic of a capitalist economy to be the anarchy of production. Harrod himself calls his theory the Antinomy Theory to contrast with the Samuelson-Hicks type theory which based on the time-lag of production. Harrod succeeds in explaining the dynamic movement of a capitalist economy by basing his theory on the essential character of capitalist investment behavior.

In the Samuelson-Hicks and Kalecki-Kaldor type models of the business cycle, the problem of the origin of business cycles is divorced from the analysis of growth, however, in Harrodian theory these two are connected systematically. In short, Harrodian theory can be called as theory of cyclical growth. On these points Harrodian theory is superior to other orthodox business cycle theories.

Despite the superiority of his theory, ultimately Harrod does not understand that the instability of the capitalist accumulation process is rooted in the productive relations of a capitalist economy. We may say that this is his limitation as an economist.

Our cycle theory, which is explained in next chapter, is constructed based on the Harrod-Okishio type investment function. At the formal level, it may be seen the same as Harrodian theory. But it differs from Harrod's qualitatively in the sense that it examines more deeply how the capitalist economy works as a system.

3.2.6 Mathematical Appendix

Hayek

Let us build a simple model of Hayek's business cycle theory. There are two sectors, production goods and consumption goods. Production goods and labour are necessary to produce consumption goods. Production goods are fixed equipment, whose useful life is unlimited. There is a time lag, or production period, between input and output. We assume this time lag to be three time periods. Employment, $N2$, and the production goods held by the consumption goods sector, K_t, in the period t determine the output of the consumption goods sector, $X3$, in the period $t+3$:

$$X_{t+3} = F(N2_t, K_t) \tag{3.80}$$

where, $\partial F/\partial N2 > 0$, $\partial^2 F/\partial N2^2 < 0$.

As the amount of production goods held by the consumption goods sector is already determined by past accumulation, when the real wage rate, R_t, is given, capitalists decide the amount of employment, $N2_t$. In order that $N2_t$ maximizes profit, it must hold that:

$$\frac{\partial F}{\partial N2_t} = R_t. \tag{3.81}$$

As R_t increases $N2_t/K_t$ decreases, and as R_t decreases $N2_t/K_t$ increases. This is what was stated above as the "Ricardo Effect".
Following from the assumption of full employment, employment by production goods sector is equal to the remainder after subtracting the employment of the consumption goods sector from the fixed total labour supply, L.

$$L = N1_t + N2_t. \tag{3.82}$$

To produce production goods, only direct labour is necessary. The amount of production goods produced, I, is determined by employment of the production goods sector, $N1$:

$$I_t = \frac{N1_t}{n} \tag{3.83}$$

where n is the amount of labour necessary to produce one unit of production goods.

All of the production goods produced are purchased by consumption goods sector and accumulated.

Suppose that laborers do not save and that they consume a certain constant ratio, b $(0 < b \leq 1)$, of the consumption goods produced. The real wage is determined by the following equation:

$$bX_t = R_t L. \tag{3.84}$$

The result of the simulation with the specified production function:

$$X_{t+3} = N2_t^{1/2} K_t^{1/2} \tag{3.85}$$

is given below.

In this simulation, the upward and downward phases of the cycle are three periods respectively. The length of the phases can differ according to the initial conditions. In all cases, the production goods sector expands and the consumption goods sector contracts hen the real wage rate is rising, and the production goods sector contracts and the consumption goods expands when the real wage rate is falling. Whether the real wage rate rises or falls in a certain period depends on whether the consumption goods sector was expanding or contracting three periods ago.

Table 3.2 Hayek's Business Cycle

period	*Real Wage*	*N2/L*	*N2/K*	*Phase*
22	2.303	0.470	0.047	
23	2.263 ↓	0.512 ↑	0.049 ↑	
24	2.210 ↓	0.562 ↑	0.051 ↑	downward phase
25	2.163 ↓	0.610 ↑	0.053 ↑	
26	2.319 ↑	0.549 ↓	0.046 ↓	
27	2.484 ↑	0.497 ↓	0.041 ↓	upward phase
28	2.639 ↑	0.458 ↓	0.036 ↓	
29	2.546 ↓	0.513 ↑	0.039 ↑	
30	2.468 ↓	0.566 ↑	0.041 ↑	downward phase
31	2.418 ↓	0.608 ↑	0.043 ↑	

Samuelson-Hicks

(Notation)
Y: income, Y_F: full-employment income, C: consumption
c: marginal propensity to consume, B: independent investment
G_b: growth rate of independent investment
γ: investment coefficient

(Model)
(Non-constrained system)
Equilibrium:

$$Y_t = C_t + I_t + B_t \tag{3.86}$$

Consumption function:

$$C_t = cY_{t-1}, \qquad 0 < c < 1 \tag{3.87}$$

Investment function:

$$I_t = \gamma(Y_{t-1} - Y_{t-2}), \qquad 0 < \gamma \tag{3.88}$$

Independent investment:

$$B_t = B_0(1 + G_b)^t \tag{3.89}$$

Substituting Eq.(3.86), (3.87), and (3.88) into Eq.(3.85), we get

$$Y_t - (c + \gamma)Y_{t-1} + \gamma Y_{t-2} - B_0(1 + G_b)^t = 0. \tag{3.90}$$

(Ceiling: full-employment)

$$Y_t = Y_F, \qquad Y_F : const. \tag{3.91}$$

(Floor: gross investment = 0)

$$Y_t - cY_{t-1} - B_0(1 + G_b)^t = 0 \tag{3.92}$$

The switching condition is summarized as follows:

$$\begin{gathered} \text{Ceiling} \Leftrightarrow Y_t \geq Y_F \\ \text{Floor} \Leftrightarrow Y_t < Y_{t-1} \\ \text{Non-constrained System} \Leftrightarrow Y_t < Y_F \text{ and } Y_t > Y_{t-1} \end{gathered}$$

Variables: Y, C, I, B
Parameters: c, γ, G_b, Y_F

(Brief explanation of the model)
If we denote Y^* as $Y_t^* = Y_0(1 + G_b)^t$ and substituting into Eq.(3.89), then

we obtain

$$\frac{Y_0}{B_0} = \frac{(1+G_b)^2}{(1+G_b)(1-c+G_b) - \gamma G_b}. \tag{3.93}$$

If the initial value and parameters satisfy Eq.(3.92), the economy grows at a constant rate. This Y^* is called as the "dynamic equilibrium income". If initial values and parameters do not satisfy Eq.(3.92), how the actual income moves depends on the characteristic roots of Eq.(3.89) (real, imaginary or the absolute value and so on).[30]

Hicks-Frisch Type model

First we analyze the following simple model of multiplier process.

$$y_t = cy_{t-1}, \qquad 0 < c < 1.$$

If we assume that investment $(= I)$, independent investment $(= B : const.)$ and denote the discrepancy from the dynamic equilibrium income $Y_t^*(= (I+B)/(1-c))$ as y_t, then we can obtain the above equation. Since c is less than unity, y_t converges to zero as time passes on.

Now assume that the economy moves on dynamic equilibrium path until period zero and from first period such random shocks as u_1, u_2, u_3 and so on are given to the system. That is, $y_0 = 0$, $y_1 = u_1$, and from second period, income are determines as follows:

$$y_2 = cy_1 + u_2$$

$$y_3 = cy_2 + u_3$$

$$y_4 = cy_3 + u_4$$

$$\cdots\cdots\cdots\cdots$$

[30] See Hicks, *op. cit.*, mathematical appendix.

Then the discrepancy from equilibrium y_t can be expressed by the stochastic difference equation:

$$y_t = cy_{t-1} + u_t, \qquad 0 < c < 1$$

where the random term have a normal distribution $N(0,1)$. If the random shocks given in this way, y_t ranges among zero and the extent of scatter do not decrease or increase. In other words, the multiplier process does not converge and "a persistent fluctuation of income" are generated. Next, we introduce a random term into Samuelson-Hicks type model. We denote the divergence from equilibrium income as y_t and the random term as u_t, then Hicks-Frisch type model can be expressed as:

$$y_t - (c+\gamma)y_{t-1} + \gamma y_{t-2} = u_t.$$

Kalecki-Kaldor Type model

(Notation)
s: marginal propensity to save
B: independent investment

(Model)
Equilibrium:

$$sY_t - A = I_t, \qquad 0 < s < 1, 0 < A \tag{3.94}$$

Investment function:
Case 1: $I_t > -dK_t$

$$I_t = aY_{t-1} - bK_t + B, \qquad 0 < a, 0 < b, 0 < B \tag{3.95}$$

Case 2: $I_t \leq -dK_t$

$$I_t = -dK_t \tag{3.96}$$

Capital Equipment:

$$K_{t+1} = K_t + I_t \tag{3.97}$$

Variables:Y, A, I, K
Parameters:s, d, a, b, A, B

Substituting Eq.(3.93) into Eq.(3.95),(3.96) and (3.97), we can summarize the system as follows:
$\underline{SystemI}$: $(I_t > -dK_t)$

In this case Y_t and K_t satisfy the following inequality:

$$\{a - s(b - d)\}Y_t - (b - d)K_t + (b - d)A + B > 0. \tag{3.98}$$

In this case the system can be reduced:

$$K_{t+1} = K_t + sY_t - A \tag{3.99}$$
$$Y_{t+1} = -\frac{b}{s}K_t + \left(\frac{a}{s} - b\right) Y_t + \frac{1}{s}\{B + (1 + b)A\}. \tag{3.100}$$

$\underline{SystemII}$: $(I_t \leq -dK_t)$

If the inequality stated above cannot be satisfied, then the system can be reduced:

$$K_{t+1} = (1 - d)K_t \tag{3.101}$$
$$Y_{t+1} = \frac{-d(1 - d)}{s}K_t + \frac{A}{s}. \tag{3.102}$$

(Brief explanation of the model)

When Y_t and K_t continue to be constant, the values are given by:

$$Y_t^* = \frac{A}{s}$$
$$K_t^* = \frac{1}{b}\left(\frac{aA}{s} + B\right).$$

Harrod Type model

(Notation)
s:marginal propensity to save
v:capital coefficient
v^*:capital coefficient under normal utilization

(Model)
Equilibrium:

$$sY_t - A = I_t, \qquad 0 < s < 1 \tag{3.103}$$

Investment function:

$$\frac{I_t}{K_t} = \frac{I_{t-1}}{K_{t-1}} + \beta(v^* - v), \qquad \beta > 0 \tag{3.104}$$

Capital coefficient:

$$v_t = \frac{K_t}{Y_t} \tag{3.105}$$

Capital accumulation:

$$K_{t+1} = K_t + I_t \tag{3.106}$$

Variables: Y, I, K, v
parameters: s, β, v^*

(Reduced form of system)

If we denote the rate of accumulation $g_t(\equiv I_t/K_t)$, we can obtain from Eq.(3.104) and (3.106)

$$v_t = \frac{K_t}{Y_t} = s\frac{K_t}{I_t} = \frac{s}{g_{t-1}}. \tag{3.107}$$

Substituting Eq.(3.106) into (3.103), then we get

$$g_t = g_{t-1} + \beta(v^* - v). \tag{3.108}$$

(Brief explanation of the model)
If $v_{t-1} = v^*$, from Eq.(3.106) and (3.107),

$$g_{t-1} = g_t = g^*.$$

And the capital equipments are utilized normally and the rate of accumulation is constant g^*.
If v_{t-1} is not equal to v^*, the following equation holds.

$$\frac{dg_t}{dg_{t-1}} = 1 + \beta\frac{s}{(g_{t-1})^2} > 1.$$

Therefore, once g_t diverges from g^*, it diverges cumulatively.

3.2.7 Programs

```
10 '* * * * * * * * * * * * * * * * *
20 ' Schumpeter model
30 '* * * * * * * * * * * * * * * * *
40 PERIOD=50
50 DIM X1(PERIOD),X2(PERIOD),N1(PERIOD)
60 DIM N2(PERIOD),K2(PERIOD),I(PERIOD)
70 DIM C(PERIOD),Q(PERIOD),F$(PERIOD)
80 '
90 '* * * * * * * Parameters * * * * * * *
```

```
100 V1=.5
110 V2=.5
120 NC1=.5
130 NC2=.4
140 GAMMA=.1
150 IC=1
160 L=100
170 '
180 '* * * * * * * Initial conditions * * * * * * *
190 T=0:F$(T)="old equilibrium"
200 K2(0)=0
210 I(0)=0
220 GOSUB 400
230 '
240 '* * * * * * * computation * * * * * * *
250 PRINT "time   Boom   or   New   Equilibrium   X1 ";
    " X2   K2   I"
260 FOR T=1 TO PERIOD
270 K2(T)=K2(T - 1)+I(T - 1)
280 IF K2(T) < (V2/NC2) * L THEN GOTO 290 ELSE GOTO 330
290 F$(T)="Boom"
300 IF T=1 THEN I(T)=IC ELSE I(T)=GAMMA*X2(T - 1)
310 GOSUB 400
320 GOTO 360
330 F$(T)="New Equilibrium"
340 I(T)=0
350 GOSUB 400
360 PRINT T,F$(T),X1(T),X2(T),K2(T),I(T)
370 NEXT T
380 END
390 '
400 N2(T)=(NC2/V2) * K2(T)
410 IF N2(T) >=L THEN N2(T)=L
420 X2(T)=N2(T)/NC2
430 N1(T)=L - N2(T)
440 X1(T)=N1(T)/NC1
```

```
450 C(T)=X1(T)+X2(T) - I(T)
460 Q(T)=I(T)/(X1(T)+X2(T))
470 RETURN
```

```
10 '* * * * * * * * * * * **
20 ' Hayek model
30 '* * * * * * * * * * * **
40 PERIOD=100
50 DIM N1(PERIOD),N2(PERIOD),X2(PERIOD),K(PERIOD)
60 DIM R(PERIOD),N2K(PERIOD),N2L(PERIOD),K$(PERIOD)
70 '
80 '* * * * * * * Parameters * * * * * * *
90 ALPHA=.5
100 NC=1
110 BC=1
120 L=100
130 '
140 '* * * * * * * Initial conditions * * * * * * *
150 T=0 : K$(0)=" A"
160 K(0)=100
170 N2(0)=70
180 GOSUB 460
190 T=1 : K$(1)=" A"
200 N2(1)=70
210 K(T)=K(T - 1)+N1(T - 1)/NC
220 GOSUB 460
230 T=2 : K$(2)=" A"
240 N2(2)=70
250 K(T)=K(T - 1)+N1(T - 1)/NC
260 GOSUB 460
270 '
280 '* * * * * * * Computation * * * * * * *
290 PRINT "time   A   or   B   N2 ";
"K   R   N2/K"
300 FOR T=3 TO PERIOD
310 X2(T)=N2(T - 3)∧ ALPHA*K(T - 3)∧(1-ALPHA)
320 K(T)=K(T - 1)+N1(T - 1)/NC
330 R(T)=BC * X2(T)/L
340 N2(T)=K(T) * (ALPHA/R(T))∧(1/(1-ALPHA))
```

```
350 IF N2(T) < =L THEN 360 ELSE 390
360 K$(T)=" A"
370 GOSUB 460
380 GOTO 420
390 K$(T)=" B"
400 N2(T)=L
410 GOSUB 460
420 PRINT T;K$(T),N2(T),K(T),R(T),N2K(T)
430 NEXT T
440 END
450 '
460 N1(T)=L - N2(T)
470 N2K(T)=N2(T)/K(T)
480 N2L(T)=N2(T)/L
490 RETURN
```

```
10 '***********************
20 ' Samuelson-Hicks Model
30 '***********************
40 PERIOD=100
50 DIM Y(PERIOD),I(PERIOD),B(PERIOD)
60 '
70 '******* Parameters *******
80 CP=.8
90 GAMMA=2.5
100 YF=10000
110 GB=.03
120 B0=1
130 '
140 '******* Equilibrium *******
150 YS0=(1+GB) * (1+GB) * B0/((1+GB) * (1 - CP+GB) -
    GAMMA*GB)
160 YS1=(1+GB) * YS0
170 '
180 '******* Initial conditions *******
190 T=0
200 Y(0)=YS0
210 Y(1)=YS1+.05
220 B(0)=B0
230 B(1)=(1+GB) * B(0)
240 '
250 '******* Computation *******
260 PRINT "time    Y    "; "I    B"
270 FOR T=2 TO PERIOD
280 B(T)=(1+GB) * B(T - 1)
290 IF Y(T - 1) >Y(T - 2) THEN I(T)=GAMMA * (Y(T - 1) -
    Y(T - 2)) ELSE I(T)=0
300 Y(T)=CP * Y(T - 1)+I(T)+B(T)
310 IF Y(T) >YF THEN Y(T)=YF : I(T)=YF - CP * Y(T - 1) - B(T)
320 PRINT T,Y(T),I(T),B(T)
330 NEXT T
```

340 END

```
10 '*******************
20 ' Hicks-Frisch model
30 '*******************
40 PERIOD=110
50 DIM Y(PERIOD),Z(PERIOD),U(PERIOD)
60 '
70 '******* Parameters *******
80 CP=.8
90 GAMMA=.9
100 SDEV=1
110 MEAN=0
120 '
130 '******* Initial conditions *******
140 T=0
150 GOSUB * SHOCK
160 Y(0)=0:Z(0)=0
170 Y(1)=U(1):Z(1)=U(1)
180 '
190 '******* Computation *******
200 PRINT "time   Y(t) - Y*(t) "; "Y(t) - Y*(t) shock=0 Random
    shock "
210 FOR T=2 TO PERIOD
220 Y(T)=(CP+GAMMA) * Y(T - 1) - GAMMA * Y(T - 2)+U(T)
230 Z(T)=(CP+GAMMA) * Z(T - 1) - GAMMA * Z(T - 2)
240 PRINT T,Y(T),Z(T),U(T)
250 NEXT T
260 END
270 '
280 * SHOCK
290 RANDOMIZE
300 FOR I=1 TO INT((PERIOD - 1)/2)+1
310 R1=RND(1) : R2=RND(1)
320 S1=SDEV * SQR( - 2 * LOG(R1))
330 S2=2 * 3.14159 * R2
340 X1=S1 * COS(S2)+MEAN
```

```
350 X2=S1 * SIN(S2)+MEAN
360 U(2 * I - 1)=X1 : U(2 * I)=X2
370 NEXT I
380 RETURN
```

```
10 '**********************
20 ' Kalecki-Kaldor model
30 '**********************
40 PERIOD=30
50 DIM Y(PERIOD),I(PERIOD),K(PERIOD)
60 '
70 '******* Parameters *******
80 SP=.2
90 COEFA=.3
100 COEFB=.5
110 A=10
120 B=10
130 D=.05
140 '
150 '******* Equilibrium *******
160 YS=A/SP
170 KS=(COEFA * A/SP+B)/COEFB
180 PRINT "Y * =";YS
190 PRINT "K * =";KS
200 '
210 '******* Initial conditions *******
220 T=0
230 Y(0)=YS - 16.5
240 K(0)=KS+16.5
250 I(0)=sp * Y(0) - A
260 IF I(0) < - D * K(0) THEN I(0)=-D * K(0):Y(0)=(I(0)+A)SP
270 '
280 '******* Computation *******
290 PRINT "time    Y    "; "K    I"
300 FOR T=1 TO PERIOD
310 K(T)=K(T - 1)+I(T - 1)
320 I(T)=COEFA * Y(T - 1) - COEFB * K(T)+B
330 IF I(T) < - D *K(T) THEN I(T)= - D * K(T)
340 Y(T)= (I(T)+A)/SP
350 PRINT T,Y(T),K(T),I(T)
```

```
360 NEXT T
370 END
```

```
10 '*************
20 ' Harrod model
30 '*************
40 PERIOD=30
50 DIM G(PERIOD),Y(PERIOD),K(PERIOD)
60 '
70 '******* Parameters *******
80 SP=.1
90 VS=2.5
100 BETA=.001
110 '
120 '******* Equilibrium *******
130 GS=SP/VS
140 '
150 '******* Initial conditions *******
160 G0=1.05
170 G(0)=G0 * GS
180 K(0)=100 : Y(0)=G(0) * K(0)/SP
190 '
200 '******* Computation *******
210 PRINT "time    g "; "K    Y"
220 FOR T= 1 TO PERIOD
230 G(T)=G(T - 1)+BETA * (VS - SP/G(T - 1))
240 K(T)=(1+G(T - 1)) * K(T - 1)
250 Y(T)=G(T) * K(T)/SP
260 PRINT T,G(T),K(T),Y(T)
270 NEXT T
280 END
```

Chapter 4

Basic Model of Business Cycle

4.1 The One Sector Basic Model

4.1.1 Temporary Equilibrium of the Real Wage Rate, the Rate of Profit and the Rate of Capital Utilization

In the capitalist economy, decisions on production are retained exclusively by the capitalist class. Capitalists decide to produce only when they expect to receive sufficient profit from production. In a competitive economy, individual capitalists consider prices (his own product price, the nominal wage rate, W, and the intermediate input price) to be beyond their control.

The set of prices which admit profit depend on the available technology. Since a one commodity economy is discussed in this section, the set of prices is composed of the commodity price, P, and the nominal wage rate, W. Then, the level of profit depends on the real wage rate, $R(= W/P)$ and the technology available for the individual capitalist, which is represented by the capital coefficient, X_i/K_i, and the labour coefficient, N_i/X_i. Since available technology differs among capitalists, some capitalists can operate their capital with a positive profit but others cannot. The higher the real wage rate, R, the fewer capitalists can operate at a positive profit. Therefore, the ratio of total output to existing capital in the whole economy, X/K, is a decreasing function of the real wage rate R. Hereafter, we denote this ratio, X/K, as $\sigma\delta$. σ is the normal capital coefficient which is independent from the real wage rate, R. δ is the rate of capital utilization and is a function of the real wage rate ($\delta = \delta(R)$).

The rate of profit, r, is defined as:

$$r = \frac{PX - WN}{PK} = (1 - Rn)\sigma\delta(R) = r(R) \tag{4.1}$$

where n is the labour coefficient, N/X. Since the rate of profit and the rate of capital utilization, δ, move in the same direction as the changes in the real wage rate, R, we can rewrite the rate of capital utilization as an increasing function of the rate of profit).[1]

$$\delta = \delta(r), \qquad 0 < \frac{d\delta/\delta}{dr/r} < 1 \tag{4.2}$$

The demand side of the economy consists of consumption demands by workers and capitalists and of investment demand. The workers consume all of their wage income, $Rn\sigma\delta K$. The capitalists consume certain amount, A, independent of their profit income. The amount of investment, I, the behavior of which is discussed later, is also independent of the current level of production. Therefore, the demand for goods becomes:

$$Rn\sigma\delta K + A + I.$$

The level of production is determined by the point where demand meets supply. At that point, the real wage rate, R, is determined. Our model is:

$$\delta(r)\sigma K = Rn\delta(r)\sigma K + A + I \tag{4.3}$$
$$r = (1 - Rn)\delta(r)\sigma. \tag{4.4}$$

From equations (4.3) and (4.4), we get:

$$rK = (1 - Rn)\delta(r)\sigma K = A + I$$

This equation says that the capitalists' demand, $A + I$, determines the level of profit, rK.
The level of real wage rate, R, depends on several variables. The larger the

[1] From this derivation of the δ function, the employment coefficient, n, is also a function of δ. But we ignore this and avoid the complication.

capitalists' demand, $A + I$, the higher the rate of profit, r, becomes, and the higher the real wage rate, R, becomes lower. If we take the capitalists' demand, $A+I$, as given, the higher labour productivity, $1/n$, and the higher the capital coefficient, σ, the larger the real wage rate, R, becomes. Besides, if the capitalists' supply behavior (the functional form of $\delta(r)$) shifts downwards, the real wage rate will drop.

4.1.2 The Investment Function, Equilibrium Growth and the Cumulative Process of Disequilibrium

The amount of investment changes over time. Investment is determined mainly by expectations of demand, which are formed by individual capitalists without any prior consultation with each other.

If the expectations of the growth of demand shift upwards, capitalists will raise the growth rate of the capital stock, $g_t - d$, (where $g = I/K$ is the rate of capital accumulation and d is the rate of depreciation) and vice versa. Although the formation of expectations is not easy to formulate, we assume that when the current rate of capital utilization, δ, is high, demand expectations are revised upwards, and vice versa. The normal rate of capital utilization, δ^*, can be defined as the rate which does not change demand expectations. By taking proper unit of capital coefficient (σ), the normal rate of capital utilization is redefined as unity. Then our gross investment function is:

$$g_t = g_{t-1} + \beta(\delta_{t-1} - 1).$$

Assuming that the capitalists' independent consumption demand grows at a constant rate, G_a, the dynamic model is as follows:

$$\delta(r_t)\sigma = R_t n\delta(r_t)\sigma + \frac{A_t}{K_t} + g_t \tag{4.5}$$

$$r_t = (1 - R_t n)\delta(r_t)\sigma \tag{4.6}$$

$$g_t = g_{t-1} + \beta(\delta_{t-1} - 1) \tag{4.7}$$

$$\frac{A_t}{K_t} = \frac{A_{t-1}}{K_{t-1}} \frac{1 + G_a}{1 + g_{t-1} - d} \tag{4.8}$$

In this model, the economy is operating satisfactorily for capitalists when commodities are sold at the normal rate of capital utilization. When the rate of capital utilization, δ, is unity, capitalists do not change the rate of capital accumulation, g. Moreover, if the rate of capital accumulation is consistent with the growth of capitalists' independent consumption demand, ($g = G_a + d$), the equilibrium can be maintained. Then the conditions for equilibrium growth are:

$$\delta(r^*) = 1 \tag{4.9}$$
$$r^* = (1 - R^* n)\sigma \tag{4.10}$$
$$g^* = G_a + d \tag{4.11}$$
$$\left(\frac{A}{K}\right)^* = r^* - (G_a + d) \tag{4.12}$$

The equilibrium condition is economically meaningful only when the equilibrium rate of profit, r^*, is higher than the equilibrium rate of capital accumulation ($r^* > g^* = G_a + d$). Otherwise, the economy experiences a commodity shortage and equilibrium is lost.

The equilibrium condition cannot be satisfied automatically, since the investment decision is carried out by individual capitalists without any prior coordination. If we neglect capitalists' independent consumption demand ($A = 0$), a high rate of capital accumulation, g, causes a high rate of capital utilization, δ, and a high rate of profit, r, this leads to an even higher rate of capital accumulation because demand expectations are revised upwards. Thus one can easily comprehend the system is unstable. We hereafter refer to this unstable movement, either upward or downward, the cumulative process of disequilibrium.

Even if we include the capitalists' independent consumption demand, the system continues to be unstable. Although in the former case ($A = 0$), there is no possibility to reverse the cumulative process of disequilibrium, if $A > 0$, a change in the ratio of capitalists' independent consumption demand to the capital stock, A/K, may reverse the cumulative disequilibrium process. However, the upward cumulative process of disequilibrium will never reverse if the rate of capital accumulation is higher than the equilibrium rate of profit ($g > r^*$).

4.1.3 The Business Cycle

The cumulative process cannot be allowed to continue if the capitalist system is to be maintained. In other words, the cumulative process must eventually be reversed in order for the capitalist system to preserve itself.

As the downward cumulative process of disequilibrium continues, the quantity of unemployed labour keeps increasing. If this situation persists the capitalist system loses its foundation.

On the other hand, if the upward cumulative process of disequilibrium continues for a very long time, investment demand relative to output keeps increasing and the share of wage goods produced keeps decreasing. Workers sell their labour in order to buy the consumption goods to enable them to live at a certain level. Therefore, they lose their incentive to supply their labour to the capitalist class, when the amount of consumption goods purchasable with their wages decreases to near zero. The resulting shortage of labour makes it impossible to continue the upward cumulative process.

Thus, both the upward and downward cumulative process of disequilibrium cannot continue forever without destroying the conditions for the reproduction of wage workers. To maintain the capitalist system, the cumulative process of disequilibrium must be reversed before it threatens the system.

In this and the next sections, we will describe the most extreme form of the business cycle. That is, the upward cumulative process of disequilibrium reverses itself because of full employment, and the downward cumulative process of disequilibrium reverses itself because of zero gross investment and capitalists' independent consumption demand. In the downward cumulative process of disequilibrium, the rate of accumulation is decreasing.

The rate of accumulation, g, stops decreasing at some point, since it cannot be negative. Although the rate of capital utilization, δ, also stops decreasing capitalists still feel there exists surplus capacity because the rate of capital utilization is below unity. The capital stock decreases only at the rate of capital depreciation, d. On the other hand, capitalists keep increasing their independent consumption demand at a non-negative rate, G_a. In this phase, the output level is equal to the sum of capitalists' consumption, A, and the amount of labour's consumption which is necessary to produce the capitalists' consumption goods.

Due to an increase in the capitalists' independent consumption demand and the decrease in capital stock, the rate of capital utilization, δ, gradually increases. When the rate of capital utilization exceeds unity, capitalists begin to accumulate again, and the phase turns into the upward cumulative process of disequilibrium.

In the upward cumulative process of disequilibrium, the employment level rises along with output. Since the rate of accumulation, g, increases exponentially, the growth rate of employment also increases. In the earlier phase of the upward process, the labour supply, L, is large relative to the level of employment. As the growth rate of employment increases and exceeds the growth rate of the labour supply, G_n, unemployed labour begins to be absorbed. Eventually, there is no unemployed labour.

Even when the economy enters the full employment phase, individual capitalists will accelerate accumulation because they feel a shortage of capital equipment relative to demand. Capitalists try to accumulate more in spite of the fact that the supply of commodities is constrained by the labour supply. Since there exists excess supply in the commodity market, some demand must be unfulfilled.

To take an extreme case, we assume that the consumption demand of labour and capitalists are suppressed and investment demand is fully satisfied. Under this assumption, investment demand is determined by the investment function described above.

On the other hand, the output level is determined by the labour supply which grows at the growth rate of labour supply, G_n, and is independent of the demand level. As the rate of capital utilization, δ, is determined by the output level and the capital stock, the rate of capital utilization increases when growth rate of output is higher than that of the capital stock ($G_n > g - d$), and vice versa.

At the point when the economy reaches the full employment level, the rate of accumulation, g, is increasing if the rate of capital utilization, δ, is higher than unity. Since the rate of accumulation increases, the growth rate of the capital stock becomes higher than that of the labour supply ($G_n < g - d$), and then the rate of capital utilization, δ, begins to decrease.

When the rate of capital utilization becomes less than unity, the rate of accumulation begins to decline. The fall in the rate of accumulation continues as long as the rate of capital utilization is below unity.

Although this process is analogous to the Goodwin's growth cycle model,[2] there are several differences between two. Firstly, Goodwin's model describes an economy where unemployed labour exists, while ours describes the full employment economy.

Secondly, the real wage rate, R, is determined by the wage equation in the labour market, in the Goodwin's model, while, in our model, the real wage rate is determined so as to clear the commodity market. Thirdly, and most importantly, Goodwin's model has no investment function, while ours has.

The economy remains in full employment, as long as demand is larger than the output which is constrained by the labour supply. As investment demand declines, the excess demand under full employment decreases. When the demand becomes smaller than the level necessary to keep the economy at the full employment, the economy returns to the underemployed state again. If the rate of capital utilization is below unity at the time, the rate of accumulation continues to decrease and the economy has now entered the downward cumulative process of disequilibrium. The model described above is summarized as follows:

(S1) The Basic Model

$$g_t = g_{t-1} + \beta(\delta_{t-1} - 1) \quad if \quad g_t < 0 \quad then \quad g_t = 0 \tag{4.13}$$

$$\frac{A_t}{K_t} = \frac{A_{t-1}}{K_{t-1}} \frac{1 + G_a}{1 + g_{t-1} - d} \tag{4.14}$$

$$\delta_t = \delta(r_t) \tag{4.15}$$

$$\sigma\delta(r_t) = R_t n \sigma\delta(r_t) + g_t + \frac{A_t}{K_t} \tag{4.16}$$

$$r_t = (1 - R_t n)\sigma\delta(r_t) \tag{4.17}$$

$$\frac{L_t}{K_t} = \frac{L_{t-1}}{K_{t-1}} \frac{1 + G_n}{1 + g_{t-1} - d} \tag{4.18}$$

[2]See R.M.Goodwin, "A Growth Cycle,", in C.H.Feinstein (ed.), *Socialism, Capitalism and Economic Growth*, Cambridge: Cambridge University Press, 1967 and section 1 of Chapter 3.

$$e_t = \frac{n\sigma\delta_t}{L_t/K_t} \tag{4.19}$$

(S2) The Full Employment Model

$$
\begin{aligned}
g_t &= g_{t-1} + \beta(\delta_{t-1} - 1) \qquad if \quad g_t < 0 \quad then \quad g_t = 0 && (4.20)\\
\frac{A_t}{K_t} &= \frac{A_{t-1}}{K_{t-1}} \frac{1 + G_a}{1 + g_{t-1} - d} && (4.21)\\
\delta_t &= \frac{L_t/K_t}{n\sigma} && (4.22)\\
R_t &= \frac{\sigma\delta_t - (g_t + (A/K_t)}{L/K_t} && (4.23)\\
r_t &= (1 - R_t n)\sigma\delta_t && (4.24)\\
\frac{L_t}{K_t} &= \frac{L_{t-1}}{K_{t-1}} \frac{1 + G_n}{1 + g_{t-1} - d} && (4.25)\\
e_t &= 1 && (4.26)
\end{aligned}
$$

$$
\begin{array}{lll}
(S1) \Longrightarrow (S2) & \text{if} & e_t > 1 \\
(S1) \Longleftarrow (S2) & \text{if} & \delta(r_t) < \delta_t
\end{array}
$$

The first equation (4.13, 4.20) is the investment function. The rate of accumulation, g, increases if the previous rate of capital utilization, δ_{t-1}, is larger than unity, and vice versa. The third to the fifth equations (4.15, 4.16, 4.17, 4,22, 4.23, 4.24) determine the rate of capital utilization, δ, the rate of profit, r, and the real wage rate, R. Under the basic model, these three variables are determined so as to clear the commodity market. On the other hand, in the full employment model, the rate of capital utilization, δ, is determined by the labour supply relative to the capital stock (4.22), the real wage rate, R, is determined so as to clear the commodity market (4.23).

The second equation (4.14, 4.22) and the sixth equation (4.18, 4.25) describe the movement of the ratio of capitalists' independent consumption demand to the capital stock, A/K, and the ratio of labour supply to capital stock, L/K, respectively. The seventh equation (4.19, 4.26) is a definition of the employment ratio (1− the unemployment ratio). The economy follows the basic model only in underemployment. When the labour market reaches full employment, the economy follows the full employment model. The full employment model prevails only when the rate of capital utilization, δ, which is restricted by the labour supply, is lower than the rate desired by capitalists ($\delta_t < \delta(r_t)$).

Our models have the following properties:
1) The equilibrium growth path of the basic model is unstable.
2) The downward process reverses due to the arresting of the decline in accumulation and the existence of capitalists' independent consumption demand.
3) The upward process reverses itself due to the limitations of the labour supply.

How the pattern of the cycle change over many repeated cycles? The size of the cycle is determined by the ceiling (full employment level) and the floor (capitalists' independent consumption). If the growth rate of capitalists' independent consumption demand, G_a, is lower (higher) than the growth rate of labour supply ($G_a < G_n$), then the difference between the ceiling and the floor gradually becomes wider (narrower). In the special case where G_n equals G_a, the difference between the ceiling and the floor remains constant. We consider this special case below.

We assume that, at the start of the initial period, the economy is at point A in Figures 4.1 and 4.2, where unemployed labour exists, the rate of accumulation, g, is positive but lower than the growth rate of labour supply, G_n, and the rate of capital utilization, δ, is unity. Since the growth rate of the capital stock is lower than the growth rate of capitalists' independent consumption demand ($g - d < G_a$), the capitalists' independent consumption demand increases relative to the capital stock, and then the rate of capital utilization, δ, increases.

Figure 4.1

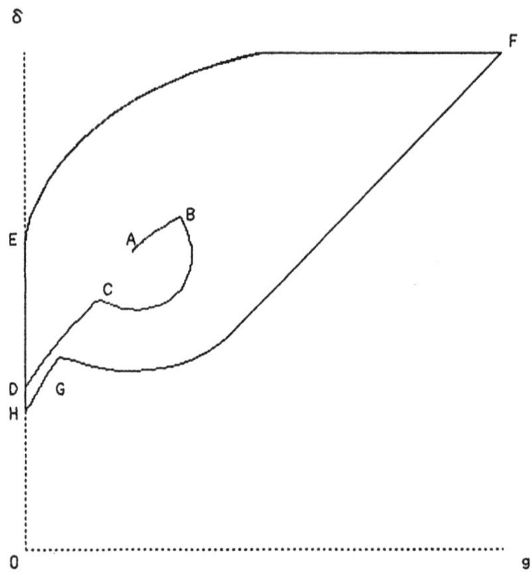

Figure 4.2

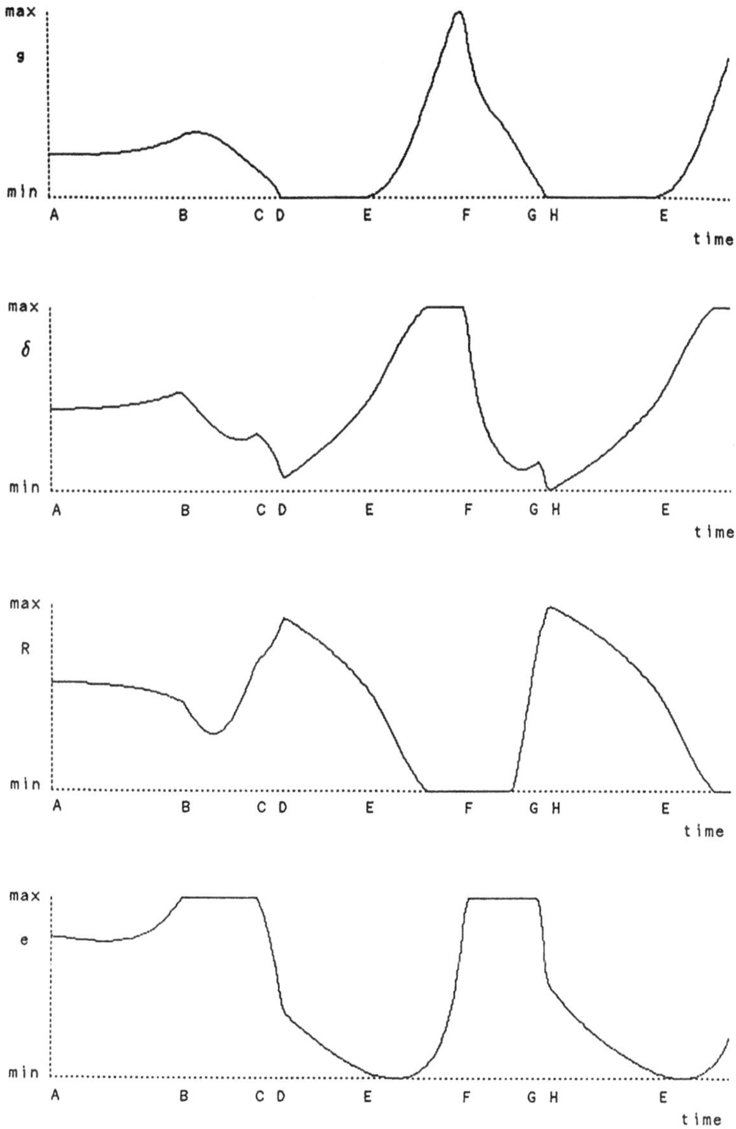
max
g
min
A B C D E F G H E
time
max
δ
min
A B C D E F G H E
time
max
R
min
A B C D E F G H E
time
max
e
min
A B C D E F G H E
time

When the rate of capital utilization, δ, becomes greater than unity, capitalists begin to increase the rate of accumulation, g. In the phase where both the rate of accumulation and the ratio of capitalists' independent consumption demand to capital stock, A/K, increase, the rate of capital utilization, δ, and the rate of profit, r, increase, while the real wage rate, R, decreases. Although the employment ratio, e, declines in the early part of this phase, it rises as the rate of accumulation increases.

When the growth rate of the capital stock becomes higher than that of capitalists' independent consumption demand ($g - d > G_a$), the ratio of capitalists' independent consumption demand to capital stock, A/K, becomes smaller, which is a negative factor for the rate of capital utilization, δ, and the rate of profit, r. In spite of this, the rate of capital utilization and the rate of profit continue to rise, due to an increase in the rate of accumulation. The employment rate, e, also increases.

When the employment rate reaches unity, the economy enters the full employment phase (point B). Output is determined by the labour supply constraint. Because the growth rate of the capital stock is higher than that of labour supply ($G_n < g - d$), the rate of capital utilization, δ, decreases. As long as the rate of capital utilization is higher than unity, the rate of accumulation, g, still increases and excess demand ($\delta(r) - \delta > 0$) becomes larger. When the rate of capital utilization reaches unity, the rate of accumulation begins to decrease. As long as the growth rate of capital stock is higher than that of labour supply ($G_n < g - d$), the rate of capital utilization continues to decrease. While the excess demand ($\delta(r) - \delta > 0$) increases in the early part of the full employment phase, it decreases as the rate of accumulation and the rate of capital utilization decrease. Although the rate of capital utilization increases again when the growth rate of the capital stock is lower than that of labour supply ($G_n > g - d$), the excess demand finally disappears due to the decrease in the rate of accumulation, and then the economy moves into the unemployment phase (point C).

In this downward process (point C to point D), the rate of accumulation continues to decrease, because the rate of capital utilization is below unity. Since the decrease in the rate of accumulation overcomes the increase in the capitalists' independent consumption demand, the rate of capital utilization and the rate of profit decrease, while the real wage rate increases. The employment rate decreases.

When the rate of accumulation falls reaches zero (point D), it stops decreasing and the downward process comes to an end. The rate of capital utilization increases due to the increase in capitalists' independent consumption demand and the depreciation of the capital stock. In this phase (point D to point E), the rate of profit increases, the real wage rate decreases and the employment rate decreases.

When the rate of capital utilization becomes greater than unity, the rate of accumulation begins to increase and the upward process starts again. The cycle which starts from point e (zero investment and a rate of capital utilization equal to unity ($g = 0$, δ=1)) returns to the same point, through the underemployed upward process (point E to point F), the full employment phase (point F to point G), the underemployed downward process (point G to point H) and the stagnation phase (point H to point E). The cycle has the same path trajectory hereafter.

4.2 The Two Sector Basic Model

In the previous section, we examined the single commodity case. Now we consider the economy where two kinds of commodities are produced: capital goods (subscript 1) and consumption goods (subscript 2). This consideration is necessary to analyze the relationship between the sectors in each phase.

4.2.1 Temporary Equilibrium of the Real Wage Rate, the Rate of Profit and the Rate of Capital Utilization in the Two Sector Model

The production activities of each sector require both labour and capital, as was assumed in the previous section. Given the amount of capital stock in each sector, output is determined according to the supply function and employment is proportional to the output level.

The rate of profit in each sector, r_1 and r_2 is defined as:

$$r_1 = \frac{P_1X_1 - WN_1}{P_1K_1} = (1 - R_1n_1)\sigma_1\delta_1(r_1)$$
$$r_2 = \frac{P_2X_2 - WN_2}{P_1K_2} = \frac{R_1}{R_2}(1 - R_2n_2)\sigma_2\delta_2(r_2).$$

The rate of capital utilization is an increasing function of each sector's own rate of profit: $\delta_1 = \delta_1(r_1)$ and $\delta_2 = \delta_2(r_2)$ respectively. The rate of profit in the capital goods sector, r_1, is a decreasing function of the real wage rate in terms of capital goods, $R_1(= W/P_1)$. On the other hand, the rate of profit in the consumption goods sector, r_2, is determined not only by the real wage rate in terms of consumption goods, $R_2(= W/P_2)$, but also by the relative price between the two commodities, $P_1/P_2(= R_2/R_1)$, and therefore also by the real wage rate in terms of capital goods, R_1. The real wage rate in terms of consumption goods, R_2, decreases the rate of profit in the consumption goods sector, r_2, while the real wage rate in terms of the capital goods sector, R_1, increases it.

The demand for the capital goods sector is the sum of the investment demand from each sector, $I_1 + I_2$, and the demand for consumption goods is the sum of consumption by capitalists and workers, $A + W(N_1 + N_2)/P_2$. The markets clearing conditions are:

$$X_1 = I_1 + I_2$$
$$X_2 = R_2(N_1 + N_2) + A.$$

Given the demand by capitalists, $I_1 + I_2$ and A, the real wage rates in terms of the two goods, R_1 and R_2 are determined so as to clear these conditions. More precisely, the real wage rate in terms of capital goods, R_1 is a decreasing function only of the investment demand, $I_1 + I_2$. Therefore, the rate of profit, r_1, and the rate of capital utilization in the capital goods sector, δ_1, increase when investment demand increases.

The real wage rate in terms of consumption goods, R_2, is a decreasing function of both investment demand and capitalists' independent consumption demand. The increase in capitalists' independent consumption demand, A, raises the rate of profit, r_2, and the rate of capital utilization in the consumption goods sector, δ_2.

The movement of the rate of profit and the rate of capital utilization in the consumption goods sector, during an increase in investment demand, is not as uncomplicated as the movement of those variables in the capital goods sector. The increase in employment in the capital goods sector, N_1, is beneficial for the profit rate in the consumption goods sector, r_2, while the decrease in the real wage rate in terms of capital goods, R_1, which accompanies the employment increase is an adverse factor for the increase in the rate of profit in the consumption goods sector.

If the former effect is greater (smaller) than the latter, the rate of profit and the rate of capital utilization in the consumption goods sector when the investment demand increase (decrease). The former effect offsets the latter, if the elasticity of the rate of capital utilization with respect to the rate of profit in the consumption goods sector, $(d\delta_2/\delta_2)/(dr_2/r_2)$, or if the ratio of capital stock in the consumption goods sector to that of the capital goods sector, K_2/K_1, are high enough.

The possibility of the consumption goods sector's profit rate declining due to an increase in investment demand shows that a so-called "under consumption crisis" may occur.[3]

The overall rate of profit, r, is the ratio of total profit to total capital stock, $K_1 + K_2$. The profit of each sector is:

$$P_1X_1 - WN_1 = I_1 + I_2 - WN_1$$
$$P_2X_2 - WN_2 = W(N_1 + N_2) + P_2A - WN_2 = WN_1 + P_2A.$$

Then the total profit in terms of capital goods can be written:

$$X_1 + \frac{P_2}{P_1}X_2 - \frac{W}{P_1}(N_1 + N_2) = I_1 + I_2 + \frac{P_2}{P_1}A$$

and the overall rate of profit, r, is:

$$r = g + \frac{P_2}{P_1}\frac{A}{K_1 + K_2}$$

[3]We shall consider "under-consumption crisis" in section 3 of this chapter

where g is the overall rate of accumulation. The increase in the overall rate of accumulation decreases the relative price, P_2/P_1. If this effect is large enough, the increase in the overall rate of accumulation decreases the overall rate of profit as a whole.

4.2.2 Equilibrium Growth and the Cumulative Process of Disequilibrium

The capitalists' independent consumption demand grows at the constant rate, G_a, and the investment function is same as in the previous section.

The desirable condition for capitalists is that commodities are sold at the normal rate of capital utilization:

$$\delta_1 K_1 = I_1 + I_2 = g_1 K_1 + g K_2$$
$$\delta_2 K_2 = R_2(n_1\sigma_1 K_1 + n_2\sigma_2 K_2) + A.$$

To satisfy this condition, both investment demand and the capitalists' independent consumption demand must be of the appropriate size relative to the capital stock of each sector. Further, the rate of accumulation in each sector, g_1 and g_2 respectively, must be equal to the $g(= g_1 = g_2 = G_a)$ to satisfy the normal capital utilization in the consumption goods sector. The ratio of capital stock between sectors, K_2/K_1, is determined so as to satisfy the normal rate of capital utilization in the capital goods sector.

Under these conditions, the rate of profit and the rate of accumulation in each sector, as well as the real wage rate in terms of each good, R_1 and R_2, and the ratio of capital stock between sectors, K_2/K_1, all remain constant, and the economy grows at the same rate as the capitalists' independent consumption demand.

Now we consider the case where the economy is off the equilibrium growth path. At first, we neglect the capitalists' independent consumption demand. The overall rate of profit is equal to the overall rate of accumulation ($r = g$). The increase in the overall rate of accumulation raises the overall rate of profit. In the capital goods sector, the increase in the rate of profit, r_1, increase rate of accumulation, g_1. On the other hand, the rate of profit in the consumption goods sector, r_2, can move in either direction.

If the rate of profit in the consumption goods sector, r_2, moves in the same direction as the profit rate of the capital goods sector, r_1, it is clear that the economy has a tendency to depart from the equilibrium path.

If the rate of profit in the consumption goods sector moves opposite to the profits of the capital goods sector, the rate of capital utilization in the consumption goods sector, δ_2, declines and the rate of accumulation, g_2, also tends to decline.

But the overall rate of profit, r, moves in the same direction as the overall rate of accumulation, g, since the extent of the decline in the rate of profit in the consumption goods sector is small. The rise of the rate of accumulation in the capital goods sector, g_1, overcomes the fall of the rate of accumulation in the consumption goods sector, g_2.

In these circumstances a positive feedback mechanism holds: the increase in the rate of accumulation, g, leads to an increase in the rate of profit, r, which leads to an increase in the rate of accumulation, g. Consequently, the discrepancy between the rates of accumulation in both sectors ($g_2 - g_1 < 0$) becomes larger.

The capital stock ratio between the sectors, K_2/K_1, declines and the movement of economy is determined by the movement of the capital goods sector, and regardless of the changes in the consumption goods sector. Next, we take into account the existence of capitalists' independent consumption demand. The positive feedback mechanism holds completely once again provided there is no reverse movement in the rates of profit of both sectors, or provided that capitalists independent consumption demand is not too large relative to the capital stock.

If there is a reversal in the relationship between the profit rates of the two sectors, and the capitalists' independent consumption demand is sufficiently large, the increase in the overall rate of accumulation may decrease the overall rate of profit. In this case, the positive feedback mechanism does not entirely hold, and the economy may seem stable. But the discrepancy in the rates of accumulation between the two sectors ($g_2 - g_1 > 0$) becomes wider. We can check by numerical calculation that the rates of profit and the rates of accumulation in two sectors move cyclically away from the equilibrium path.

Therefore, the two sector model is as unstable as the one sector model. The properties of this model, determined by numerical calculation, are as follows: In the upward process, overall output and the overall rate of profit both increase. The rate of profit in the capital goods sector is larger than the rate of profit in the consumption goods sector ($r_1 > r_2$), since the demand for capital goods is large relatively. The rate of accumulation in the capital goods sector become higher than the rate of accumulation in the consumption goods sector ($g_1 > g_2$). The discrepancy in the rates of profit and accumulation between the two sectors ($r_1 > r_2, g_1 > g_2$) becomes larger. The capital stock ratio between the sectors, K_2/K_1, becomes smaller. In the downward process, these variables all move in reverse directions.

4.2.3 The Business Cycle

As was discussed in the previous section, the cumulative process of disequilibrium must be reversed in order to for the capitalist system to survive. The assumptions for the successful reversal process are the same as discussed above, that is, the upper cumulative process of disequilibrium is reversed by full employment and the downward cumulative process of disequilibrium is reversed by capitalists' independent consumption demand and non-negative investment.

Although various forms of cycle are observable in the numerical calculation, we limit ourselves to explaining the standard business cycle here (see Figure 4.3). This business cycle is a converging cycle which is reached after several ups and downs. The phases of the business cycle are classified as follows:

1) Stagnation with zero investment in both sectors.
2) The upward cumulative process induced by investment in the consumption goods sector.
3) The upward cumulative process due to investment in both sectors.
4) The downward cumulative process caused by the full employment constraint.
5) The downward cumulative process in the underemployed economy.

In the stagnation phase, with zero investment in both sectors (phase 1: *A*-*B*), consumption goods are produced due to capitalists' independent consumption demand, while capital goods are not produced. The increase in consumption demand and the decrease in the capital stock in the consumption goods sector raise the rate of capital utilization in the consumption goods sector, δ_2. When the rate of capital utilization in the consumption goods sector reaches unity, capitalists in the consumption goods sector begin to invest.

Figure 4.3

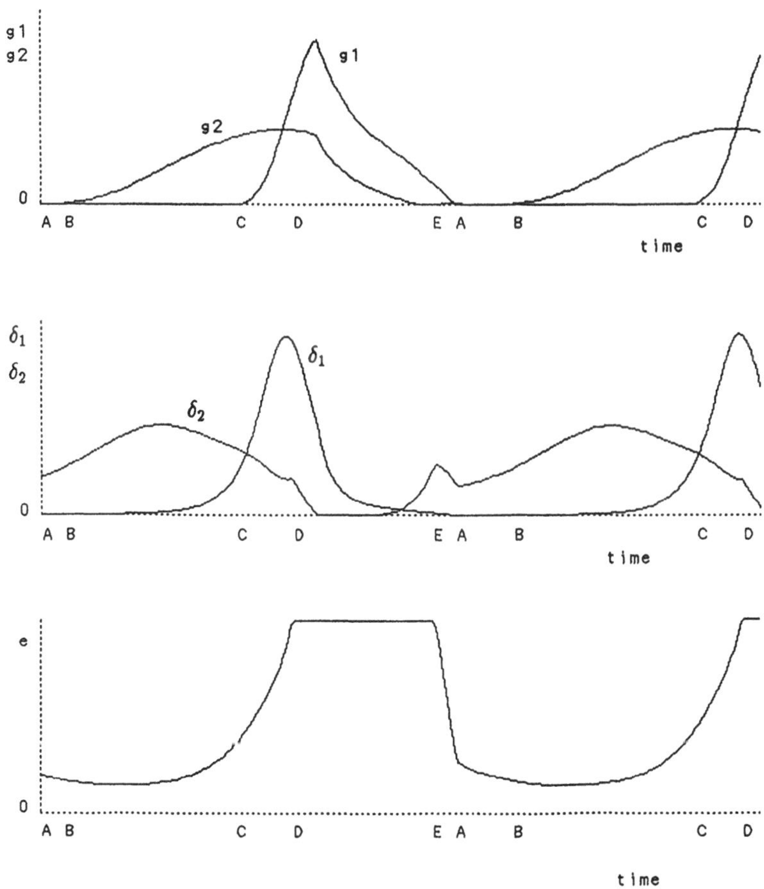

The economy then enters the next phase, that is, the upward cumulative process due to investment in the consumption goods sector (phase 2: B-C). The increase in the investment demand coming from the consumption goods sector raises the rate of capital utilization in the capital goods sector, δ_1. The relative magnitude of the consumption goods sector's investment demand, g_2K_2/K_1, may be small. But it grows due to the increase in the rate of accumulation in the consumption goods sector, g_2, and the increase in the absolute level of the capital stock in the consumption goods sector, K_2/K_1. Then the rate of capital utilization in the capital goods sector, δ_1, increases and reaches unity.

The upward cumulative process due to the investment of both sectors (phase 3: C-D) begins with investment in the capital goods sector. The rate of capital utilization in the capital goods sector increases since the investment demand in both sectors increases, while the rate of capital utilization in the consumption goods sector begins to decline. This is because the magnitude of the capitalists' independent consumption demand relative to capital stock is decreasing ($g_2 - d > G_a$). Besides, the rise in the capital goods price squeezes the rate of profit in the consumption goods sector. In spite of the decline in the rate of capital utilization in the consumption goods sector, the investment demand in both sector grows and the rate of employment, e, grows. At last, the economy enters full employment.

When the economy reaches the full employment (phase 4: D-E), capitalists cannot procure the necessary labour. The shift of labour from the consumption goods sector to the capital goods sector must occur in order to realize the investment goods production fully. As a result, the real wage rate in terms of consumption goods, R_2, declines and capitalists' independent consumption demand is restricted. When the shift of labour reaches the limit, it becomes impossible to produce all the capital goods demanded. Since the rate of accumulation in the capital goods sector is higher than the growth rate of the labour force ($g_1 - d > G_n$) at that time, the feasible rate of capital utilization ($\delta_1 < L/(n_1\sigma_1K_1)$) falls. When the rate of capital utilization in the capital goods sector reaches unity, the rate of accumulation in the capital goods sector begins to fall. The excess demand for labour begins to shrink, and a shift of labour from the capital goods sector to the consumption goods sector occurs, which makes the rise in the real wage rate in terms of consumption goods possible. When he excess demand for labour diminishes, the economy returns to underemployment.

When the economy enters the under employment phase (phase 5: E-A), the decline in the rate of accumulation in both sectors decreases employment in the capital goods sector, which decreases the consumption demand of workers. Finally, investment demand reaches zero, and the economy enters the stagnation phase (phase 1) again.

4.3 Turning Point

4.3.1 Some Reversing Factors at the Upper Turning Point

It is the nature of the capitalist economy to produce a cumulative process of disequilibrium.

If in a given period there arises an excess demand in the commodity market, which brings an over-utilization of capital equipment, then in the next period the accumulation demand increases so that the excess demand is enlarged and the equipment utilization rate goes up. In this upward disequilibrium process, prices increase faster than the money wage rate so that the real wage rate goes down and the rate of profit increases. Unless this process is reversed in time, the fall in the real wage rate destroys the reproduction of labour power. Therefore turning this upward disequilibrium process into a downward one is necessary to maintain the capitalist economy.

Conversely, in the downward disequilibrium process the excess supply is enlarged and the equipment utilization rate decreases so that the real wage rate goes up and the rate of profit falls. Unless this process is reversed in time, it makes the reproduction of labour power impossible because the increasing unemployment destroys workers' expectations of employment so that workers stop appearing on the labour market. Therefore turning this downward disequilibrium process into an upward one is also necessary to preserve the capitalist economy.

In the previous sections of this chapter it was explained that the upward disequilibrium process is reversed by full employment and the downward equilibrium process by the basic consumption demand of capitalists. However, full employment is only one of the probable reversing factors at the upper turning point of the business cycle, and likewise, the basic consumption demand is only one of the probable reversing factors in the lower turning point. It is also noted that the existence of a reversing factor does not necessarily guarantee the reversal of the cumulative process. It only means a period of reversal.

In this section we shall consider in more detail the following reversing factors: At the upper turning point, (1) a fall in the rate of profit in the consumer goods sector, (2) a bottleneck of producer goods, (3) full employment, (4) the lower limit of the real wage rate and (5) credit restriction.

At the lower turning point, (1) a rise of the profit rate in the consumer goods sector, (2) the introduction of new technology and (3) basic consumption demand.

the decline of the rate of profit in the consumer goods sector

In the upward disequilibrium process the overall rate of profit is going up. However, not every profit rate in every sectors necessarily increases. In some cases, it may happen that the profit rate in the capital goods sector goes up but the profit rate in consumer goods sector drops.

In the upward process, accumulation demand increases cumulatively so that the price of capital goods increases and the profit rate in the capital goods sector increases. Increases in output and employment in the capital goods sector bring about an increase in the demand for consumer goods so that the price of consumer goods increases.

The definition of the profit rate of the consumer goods sector, r_2, is:

$$r_2 = \frac{p_2 X_2 - w N_2}{p_1 K_2}$$

where p_2 denotes the price of consumer goods, p_1 the price of capital goods, X_2 the output of consumer goods, K_2 the capital equipment of the consumer goods sector, w the money wage rate, and N_2 the employment in the consumer goods sector.

So the profit rate in the consumer goods sector falls if the price of capital goods increases faster than the price of consumer goods. The degree of the increase in the price of capital goods depends upon the degree of the increase in accumulation demand and upon the supply behavior of the capital goods sector. It is greater, if the increase in accumulation demand is greater, and if capitalists in the capital goods sector require a greater rate of profit to expand their output. Thus, in the upward process where accumulation demand increases cumulatively, the profit rate in the consumer goods sector falls if the price of capital goods increases faster than the price of consumer goods. The fall in the profit rate brings the under utilization of capital equipment in the consumer goods sector while, at the same time, the capital equipment of the producer goods sector is being operated above the normal level. It is important to realize the possibility of this situation occurring.

According to Keynesian multiplier theory, an increase in investment brings about an increase in income and output by the multiplier. However, it does not always induce an increase in output and income in the consumer goods sector, although an increase in investment necessarily brings an increase in output and income in the producer goods sector.

In this situation, while capitalists diminish their capital accumulation demand in the consumer goods sector, they so accelerate their accumulation demand for the capital goods sector that the upward process continues. But in face of low demand from the consumer goods sector capitalists in the capital goods sector may have such pessimistic expectations of the future that they diminish capital accumulation demand. Then the overall accumulation demand declines and the upward cumulative disequilibrium is reversed.

Once the capitalists in capital goods sector diminish their accumulation demand so that the utilization of equipment falls below the normal level, then accumulation demand shrinks still more. Thus, the downward cumulative process begins. Thus, a fall in the rate of profit in the consumer goods sector causes the switching of the upward process into a downward one.

However, we note some restrictions: Firstly, there can exist a situation where the production of capital goods for the consumer goods sector decreases, but the total production of capital goods increases because the accumulation demand of the capital goods sector remains high enough to maintain the overall accumulation demand.

Secondly, as the upward process continues the utilization rate of the capital goods sector becomes very high. So that a large decrease in accumulation demand is necessary to bring about the under utilization of capital equipment and thereby switching into the downward process.

Thirdly, a decline in the utilization rate of the capital goods sector, which accompanies a decline in accumulation demand, causes a fall in the price of capital goods, so the rate of profit and the accumulation demand of the consumer goods sector recover.

Hence, capitalists in the capital goods sector come to have such optimistic expectations that they increase accumulation demand. Then the upward process is sustained and the recession is temporally avoided. This case is called an "intermediate crisis". Incidentally, "under-consumption theory" says that a crisis is caused by a shortage of consumer goods relative to production capacity. But it is not true that a boom necessarily causes underconsumption and that underconsumption necessarily causes a crisis. We can only state that underconsumption is one of the factors that causes a crisis.

A Bottleneck of Producer Goods

In the upward disequilibrium process the increase in demand for capital goods exceeds the increase in the production capacity of that sector. Sooner or later the time will come when the output of capital goods is less than the demand, even if the capital equipment is fully utilized. The construction of capital equipment takes time. When a bottleneck occurs buyers cannot satisfy all of their demand and the delivery of goods is delayed. Buyers offer a higher price to obtain goods and sellers raise prices because of the shortage. There will be unfulfilled demand remaining.

A bottleneck of producer goods depresses the production of consumer goods mainly for the two reasons. Firstly, the constriction of production in the capital goods sector is accompanied by a contraction of employment, which depresses consumption demand. Secondly, a rise in the price of capital goods causes a fall of the profit rate in the consumer goods sector which brings a low rate of capital utilization in the consumer goods sector.

Then the excess demand is sustained in the producer goods market, firms become unable to purchase producer goods. In these firms the construction of capital equipment is delayed and a part of or all of their investment become infeasible. So the capitalists are forced to reconsider their present and future investment and to diminish their accumulation demand. In fact, the capitalists in the consumer goods sector diminish their accumulation demand according to the fall in their rate of profit. These factors may force a reduction in the total accumulation demand which reverses the upward disequilibrium process into a downward one.

There are some qualifications to this explanation: firstly, A bottleneck of producer goods brings about a large excess demand so that capitalists in the capital goods sector may increase their accumulation demand still more. Secondly, the firms which cannot purchase all their ordered goods may attempt still greater accumulation for reasons of competition, rather than diminish their accumulation demand.

If the reduction in accumulation demand, which is caused by a bottleneck, is not so great that the utilization rate of capital goods remains above the normal level, then the accumulation demand of the capital goods sector increases again. In this case the recession is temporarily avoided. A disappearance of a bottleneck which accompanies a reduction of accumulation demand may bring about a fall in the price of capital goods and a rise in the profit rate of the consumer goods sector. So the accumulation demand of the consumer goods sector increases again. In this case also a recession is temporarily avoided.

Full Employment

In the upward cumulative process production and employment increase cumulatively and the rate of unemployment falls. Sooner or later full employment is reached. Under full employment it becomes impossible to increase production as a whole. Excess demand appears in the commodity market as well as in the labour market.

When an increase in employment is constrained by labour supply, in order to increase their work forces capitalists in one sector it necessary to pull out workers employed in the other sector by offering a higher money wage rate. If the capital goods sector draws workers from the consumer goods sector then the output and the rate of profit in the consumer goods sector will fall. If the reverse occurs, then the output and the rate of profit in the capital goods sector will fall. In the sector in which the rate of profit falls below the normal level capitalists diminish their accumulation demand. If this reduction is sufficiently large, then the total accumulation demand declines and the production in the capital goods sector decreases. The decrease in output of the capital goods sector is followed by a decline of employment in the same sector which leads to a decrease in consumption demand. Thus, full employment turns the upward disequilibrium process downward.

However, full employment does not necessarily always immediately reverse an upward process. There are some restrictions to be considered. When workers in the consumer goods sector are drawn off and the accumulation demand of the consumer goods sector diminishes, an upward process continues unless the accumulation demand of the capital goods sector also declines.

When workers in the capital goods sector are lost and the accumulation demand of the sector diminishes, an increase in the total demand for accumulation continues, provided the profit rate of the consumer goods sector is still high and the accumulation demand of consumer goods sector is very large.

Then the price of capital goods rises again and both the rate of profit and the rate of utilization in the capital goods sector soon recover. The firms which face a shortage of labour may increase accumulation demand still more in order to introduce labour-saving technology. It is not correct to say that the real wage rate rises under full employment because the money wage rate rises due to the excess demand in the labour market. It is because the real wage rate (the money wage rate / the price of consumer goods) depends upon prices as well as the money wage rate and prices rise also because of the excess demand in the commodity market. Now let us suppose that consumption demand comes only from workers, and that workers spend all their wages, then it follows *ex post* that under full employment:

$$\text{output of consumer goods} = \text{real wage rate} \times \text{labour supply.}$$

Therefore, if the labour supply is constant, then any decline in the output of consumer goods reduces the real wage rate. If the labour supply grows, then the real wage rate falls as long as the capital stock *per capita* increases.

This is because an increase in the capital stock it per capita requires a shift of workers from the consumer goods sector to the capital goods sector so that the rate of increase in consumer goods is less than the rate of growth of labour supply. Full employment is caused by such a strong accumulation of capital that the rate of capital growth exceeds the rate of growth of the labour supply. Therefore the real wage rate falls at least in the beginning of full employment.

This will also be true in a socialist economy, because in order to sustain a high rate of accumulation it is necessary to shift workers from the consumer goods sector to the capital goods sector. It is inevitable that output of consumer goods declines and the real wage rate falls in the process.

In a socialist economy, when he accumulation of capital ends, it is possible to shift workers from the capital goods sector to the consumer goods sector, retaining full employment. Therefore, *per capita* consumption increases. In the capitalist economy a halt in capital accumulation brings about a reduction in the demand for labour. Hence, it means the start of a downward process which is accompanied by increasing unemployment and an decline in *per capita* consumption.

The Lower Limit of the Real Wage Rate

In the upward cumulative process the real wage rate is falling. By the definition,

$$\text{real wage rate} = \text{money wage rate} \ / \ \text{price of consumer goods.}$$

In the upward process it is certain that a fall in the rate of unemployment increases the money wage rate, but prices increase relative to the money wage rate. It is because an increase in accumulation demand leads to an excess demand for consumer goods so that the price of consumer goods increases faster than the money wage rate. Now we shall consider it in detail.

Now let us suppose that the money wage rate is fixed. We shall consider the effect of an increase in investment on the real wage rate. An increase in investment increases employment in the capital goods sector. Thus, it causes an increase in the demand for consumer goods. At the same time it increases the price of capital goods and so reduces the profit rate in the consumer goods sector, which decreases the supply of consumer goods.

Such excess demand is cleared by the rise in the price of consumer goods. Therefore, the real wage rate falls.

Once the real wage falls, the prices of commodities increase proportional to the money wage rate, if the money wage rate increases. There are two points to note concerning this fact:

Firstly, the price of capital goods increases proportional to the money wage rate. Because capitalists require a certain rate of profits in order to produce the capital goods corresponding to a certain volume of investment demand. By definition, the profit rate of the capital goods sector, r_1, is:

$$r_1 = \frac{p_1 X_1 - wN_1}{p_1 K_1}.$$

where p_1 denotes the price of capital goods, w the money wage rate, X_1 the output of capital goods, K_1 the capital of the sector and N_1 the employment of the sector. When the money wage rate increases, in order to produce the same output as before and to earn the same rate of profit, it is necessary that the price of capital goods increases proportional to the money wage rate. If the price increases less than the money wage rate, then the rate of profit falls and excess demand rises. If the price increases more than the money wage rate, then the rate of profit rises and excess supply develops.

Secondly, the price of consumer goods increases proportional to the money wage rate. By the definition of the profit rate of the consumer goods sector, r_2, is:

$$r_2 = \frac{p_2 X_2 - wN_2}{p_1 K_2}$$

where p_2 is the price of consumer goods, w_2 the output of the consumer goods sector, N_2 employment in the sector, and K_2 the capital of the sector. If the price of consumer goods increases proportional to the money wage rate and the price of capital goods, then the profit rate of the consumer goods sector is the same as before and supply of output is the same. Assume that workers spend all of their wages and capitalists save all of their profit, then

$$\text{the demand for consumption} = \frac{w}{p_2}(N_1 + N_2).$$

Hence, consumption demand does not change if the price of consumer goods increases proportional to the money wage rate. Therefore an increase in prices which is proportional to the change in the money wage rate equates the demand to the supply of consumer goods. In order to maintain the reproduction of labour it is necessary that the real wage rate is greater than a certain minimum level which determined physically and socially. As inflation continues workers require an increase in the money wage to offset the increase in the cost of living. Individual capitalists do not easily submit to an increase in money wage which diminishes their profits. However, they are likely to agree to an increase in money wage, to avoid labour disputes.

When the money wage rises, as we have seen earlier, prices rise so that the real wage rate is held constant. Then workers require an additional increase in the money wage. Thus, a wage and price spiral is established.

A decline in the real wage rate reduces accumulation demand in the following two ways: Firstly, a decline in the real wage rate brings about such violent inflation that people lose confidence in the stability of the value of money.

The inflation of wages and prices makes it difficult for capitalists to form confident expectations of future prices, wages and the rate of profit. Thus they diminish their accumulation demand. Secondly, a decline in the real wage rate stimulates labour disputes about wages and salaries. Labour disputes interfere with production activities.

Output is reduced, and future production plans are modified so that accumulation demand is diminished.

If such a decline in accumulation demand arises, then output falls and a downward process begins. However, this switch does not necessarily begin. It is subject to the following restrictions:

Even with violent inflation, capitalists may not stop their accumulation demand. They may generate strong accumulation demand because inflation means excess demand in the commodity market and the going rate of profit is extraordinary high. Also, in a labour dispute, capitalists may maintain production activity by firing some workers and employing others.

Credit Restriction

An accelerated increase in accumulation demand in the upward process necessitates an acceleration in credit demand. If the supply of credit is wanting, then the rate of interest rises too much. The rise in the interest rate may diminish accumulation demand and turn the upward process downward.

But a rise in the interest rate does not necessarily bring about a decline in accumulation demand. In the upward process the realised rate of profit is growing, and so capitalists expand their accumulation demand in spite of a rise in the rate of interest. Further, the real rate of interest may decrease on account of the inflation of prices. In the upward process, the supply of credit is not always constrained. Financial resources are the savings of capitalists, bank loans, and trade credits. The savings of capitalists are certainly restricted by the realised profits. Banks tend to keep the reserve rate constant. Therefore, bank loans are restricted if the central bank is to restrict high powered money.

It is important whether or not trade credit expands. It depends upon the ability to realise commodities. In the upward process there is excess demand in commodity markets and the sale of commodities is expanding smoothly so that the repayment of credit is going well.

Suppliers of trade credit have no anxiety about the repayment of additional credit. Hence trade credit has no limitation in a time of boom. Yet, when excess supply appears in the commodity markets, the repayment of credit from sales becomes difficult. In this case, capitalists run to the bank to get financing so that the rate of interest goes up sharply.

4.3.2 The Lower turning point

A rise of the rate of profit in the consumer goods sector

In the downward cumulative process the rate of profits falls. Yet, in some cases it may happen that the profit rate in the capital goods sector falls but the profit rate in the consumer goods sector rises. This can be revised the case where the profit rate in the capital goods sector rises but the profit rate in the consumer goods sector falls in the upward process.

A cumulative decrease in accumulation demand induces excess supply and a decrease in the price of capital goods. It also leads to a reduction of output and employment in the capital goods sector, and a decline in demand and a decrease in the prices of consumer goods which tends to bring a fall in the profit rate in the consumer goods sector. However, the profit rate in the consumer goods sector rises if the price of capital goods decreases much faster than the price of consumer goods.

A rise in the profit rate of the consumer goods sector brings a rise in the utilization rate of capital equipment and an increase in accumulation demand of the consumer goods sector. On the other hand, in the capital goods sector, a fall in the rate of profit brings a low rate of utilization of capital equipment and a decrease in accumulation demand.

In the downward process, where the rate of profit in the consumer goods sector and the output of capital goods as a whole decreases, but the output of capital goods for the consumer goods sector increases.

This may encourage capitalists in the capital goods sector to have optimistic expectations about future demand and therefore increase their demand for capital accumulation. Then the overall accumulation demand expands and the utilization rate may recover to above the normal level which increases accumulation demand still more. Thus upward process starts.

However a rise in the rate of profit in the consumer goods sector does not necessarily switch the downward process into an upward one for various reasons. Although the production of capital goods for the consumer goods sector increases, the rate of utilization of capital in the capital goods sector is low in the downward process.

Therefore, capitalists in the capital goods sector do not increase their accumulation demand unless they have a extremely optimistic expectations of future demand.

As the downward process proceeds, the rate of utilization of capital equipment in the capital goods sector becomes very low. A large and continuous increase in accumulation demand is necessary in order to switch the downward process into an upward one. Some rise in the rate of utilization of the capital goods sector which follows some increase in the accumulation demand causes some rise in the price of capital goods.

Consequently, the rate of profit in the consumer goods sector is likely to fall and the accumulation demand of the consumer goods sector may decline. Then capitalists may lose their optimistic outlook and accumulation demand declines still further and the downward process persists.

The introduction of new technologies

In the downward process prices are falling faster than the money wage rate. So the real wage rate is rising and the rate of profits is falling. Firms which use lower productivity technology are forced to stop their operations. Some firms go bankrupt.

One of the main means of preventing a fall in the rate of profit is to reduce the cost of production by introducing new technologies which have a lower labour coefficients and/or a lower capital coefficients. If one capitalist introduces new technologies faster than the other, he will get a larger market share and achieve a rise in his profit. The other capitalists who fail to introduce these new technologies will lose their market.

The introduction of new technologies requires the scrapping of old equipment and the construction of new equipment which embodies the new technology. That necessitates new investment. This investment demand increases the output of capital goods. It leads to a recovery in the capital goods sector and is followed by a recovery in the consumer goods sector. However, the introduction of new technologies does not always turn the downward process into an upward one as we shall see.

The introduction of new technologies needs a large fund of investment to make possible research and to build the new capital goods. In a period of depression, many firms have already a great volume of debt.

So such firms, which are in a weak credit standing, find it difficult to make an investment and introduce new technologies.

The reduction of costs made throughout the introduction of the new technologies pushes the profit rate up if the market prices are constant. When the new equipment embodying the new technologies is operated, the increase in production capacity brings about a fall in prices and capitalists may not secure profits sufficient to utilize the capital equipment at the normal level.

In the downward process employment decreases. The introduction of new technologies, which are labour-saving, create further unemployment, and a decrease in consumption demand.

Consequently, the prices of consumer goods drop sharply and the rate of profit in the consumer goods sector even more. Then the downward process is sustained.

Incidentally, some economists maintain that, "In a depression the kind of investment is replacement investment which increases the organic composition of capital. And in a boom it is new investment to expand the volume of equipment so that the organic composition of capital is constant"[4]. This proposition is not correct, if it is taken to mean that the introduction of new technologies is limited only to a period of depression. Because even in a boom, price competition forces capitalists to introduce new technologies and to use new equipment with higher productivity. A depression and a boom are different with respect to the conditions under which old equipment, with lower productivity, is scrapped. In a depression, a rise in the real wage rate squeezes the profits of old equipment and forces its abandonment. In a boom, a fall in the real wage rate makes old equipment profitable and it may be utilized throughout its full physical life.

Basic consumption demand

As the downward process continues, accumulation demand is declining, and eventually gross investment becomes zero. Then the capital goods sector stops producing. However, consumer goods are still produced. The consumer goods sector produces its output for the basic consumption of capitalists and the consumption demands of workers employed in the sector. The consumption demand of workers diminishes as their income declines. The consumption demand of capitalists is not restricted by their profits so that they can consume at the level necessary to maintain their household.

There is a minimum level of production in the consumer goods sector corresponding to this minimum basic consumption demand of capitalists, and there is no replacement of equipment. Then the existing capital equipment depreciates and the utilization rate in the consumer goods sector goes up gradually.

Sooner or later, the rate of utilization exceeds the normal level. Then the accumulation demand of the consumer goods sector begins to increase which leads to the production of capital goods. Over the course of time

[4]K. Uno, *Theory of Crisis*, Iwanami-shoten, 1976, pp.66-77, in Japanese

the utilization rate in the capital goods sector also exceeds the normal level and the accumulation demand of the capital goods sector begins to increase. Thus, an upward process begins.

However, there are some restrictions to this process. In fact, a recovery of the consumer goods sector which accompanies capital depreciation brings about a demand for capital goods. But if a rise in the price of capital goods reduces the profit rate in the production of consumer goods, then the rate of utilization of consumer goods will drop again and the accumulation demand ceases to increase. Further it takes a very long time for the depreciation of capital that leads to a recovery. In this recovery process the level of output is very low and a high rate of unemployment continues.

Therefore, it becomes difficult to reproduce waged workers because in a long depression workers no longer expect to be employed again.

4.4 Mathematical Appendix

4.4.1 The One Sector Basic Model

(Model)
Equilibrium condition of commodity market

$$X_t = R_t N_t + I_t + A_t \tag{4.27}$$

Production techniques

$$X_t = \delta_t \sigma K_t \tag{4.28}$$

Labour demand

$$N_t = n X_t \tag{4.29}$$

the rate of profit

$$r_t = \frac{X_t - R_t N_t}{K_t} \tag{4.30}$$

Utilization function

$$\delta_t = \delta(r_t) \tag{4.31}$$

Capital accumulation

$$K_{t+1} = K_t + I_t - dK_t \tag{4.32}$$

the rate of capital accumulation

$$g_t = \frac{I_t}{K_t} \tag{4.33}$$

Investment function

$$g_{t+1} = g_t + \beta(\delta_t - 1) \tag{4.34}$$

Basic consumption

$$A_{t+1} = (1 + G_a)A_t \tag{4.35}$$

Labour supply

$$L_{t+1} = (1 + G_n)L_t \tag{4.36}$$

Endogenous variables:

$X, R, N, \delta, I, K, g, A, L$

Parameter:

$\sigma, \beta, n, G_a, G_n$

Constraint of the model:

[A] $N \leq L$
[B] $R \geq R_{min}$
[C] $g \geq 0$

From (4.27),(4.28),(4.29) and (4.33), we can obtain,

$$(1 - R_t n)\sigma\delta_t = g_t + A_t/K_t. \tag{4.37}$$

And from(4.30) we get

$$r_t = (1 - Rn)\sigma\delta_t$$

Therefore, from (4.37),

$$r_t = g_t + A_t/K_t \tag{4.38}$$

And from (4.31) we get

$$\delta_t = \delta(g_t + A_t/K_t) \tag{4.39}$$

From (4.32), (4.33) and (4.35) it follows that

$$\frac{A_{t+1}}{K_{t+1}} = \frac{1 + G_a}{1 + g_t - d}\frac{A_t}{K_t} \tag{4.40}$$

Eqs. (4.39), (4.34) and (4.40) determine the three variables, δ, g, and A/K.

(Equilibrium)

$$g^* = G_a + d$$

$$\delta(r^*) = 1$$

$$(A/K)^* = r^* - G_a - d \tag{4.41}$$

(Constrained model)

[A] $N \geq L$: output is constrained by the labour supply.

[B] $R_2 \leq R_{min}$: The value of R is set at R_{min} and the basic consumption A will be reduced.

[C] $g < 0 : g = 0$

4.4.2 The Two Sector Basic Model

Equilibrium condition of commodity market

$$X_1^t = I_1^t + I_2^t \tag{4.42}$$
$$X_2^t = R_2^t(N_1^t + N_2^t) + A^t \tag{4.43}$$

Production techniques

$$X_1^t = \delta_1^t \sigma_1 K_1^t \tag{4.44}$$
$$X_2^t = \delta_2^t \sigma_2 K_2^t \tag{4.45}$$

Labour demand

$$N_1^t = n_1 X_1^t \tag{4.46}$$
$$N_2^t = n_2 X_2^t \tag{4.47}$$

the rate of profit

$$r_1^t = \frac{X_1^t - R_1^t N_1^t}{K_1^t} \tag{4.48}$$
$$r_2^t = \frac{X_2^t - R_2^t N_2^t}{K_2^t} \frac{R_1^t}{R_2^t} \tag{4.49}$$

Utilization Function

$$\delta_1^t = \delta_1(r_1^t) \tag{4.50}$$
$$\delta_2^t = \delta_2(r_2^t) \tag{4.51}$$

Capital accumulation

$$K_1^{t+1} = K_1^t + I_1^t - d_1 K_1^t \tag{4.52}$$
$$K_2^{t+1} = K_2^t + I_2^t - d_2 K_2^t \tag{4.53}$$

the rate of capital accumulation

$$g_1^t = \frac{I_1^t}{K_1^t} \tag{4.54}$$

$$g_2^t = \frac{I_2^t}{K_2^t} \tag{4.55}$$

Investment function

$$g_1^{t+1} = g_1^t + \beta_1(\delta_1^t - 1) \tag{4.56}$$

$$g_2^{t+1} = g_2^t + \beta_2(\delta_2^t - 1) \tag{4.57}$$

Basic consumption

$$A^{t+1} = (1 + G_a)A^t \tag{4.58}$$

Labour supply

$$L^{t+1} = (1 + G_n)L^t \tag{4.59}$$

Endogenous variables:

$X_1, X_2, R_1, R_2, N_1, N_2, \delta_1, \delta_2$

$I_1, I_2, K_1, K_2, g_1, g_2, A, L$

Parameter:

$\sigma_1, \sigma_2, \beta_1, \beta_2, n_1, n_2, G_a, G_n$

(Constraint of the model)

[A] $N_1 + N_2 \leq L$

[B] $R_2 \geq R_{min}$

[C] $g_1, g_2 \geq 0$

[D] $\delta_1 \leq \delta_{1max}$

From (4.42),(4.43),(4.46) and (4.48), we can obtain,

$$\delta_1 = \frac{g_1 + g_2\lambda}{\sigma_1} \tag{4.60}$$

$$r_1 = (1 - R_1 n_1)\sigma_1\delta_1 \tag{4.61}$$

These equations and (4.50) suffice to determine the values of δ_1, r_1, and R_1 if the values, g_1, g_2, and λ, are given.
From (4.43), (4.45), (4.47) and (4.49), we obtain

$$\lambda(1 - R_2 n_2)\sigma_2\delta_2 = R_2 n_1 \sigma_1 \delta_1 + \frac{A}{K_2}\lambda \tag{4.62}$$

$$r_2 = (1 - R_2 n_2)\sigma\delta_2\frac{R_1}{R_2}. \tag{4.63}$$

From these two equations, (4.51) and (4.60),

$$\frac{\sigma_2\delta_2(r_2)(\lambda r_2 - R_1 n_1 \sigma_1 \delta_1)}{r_2 + R_1 n_2 \sigma_2 \delta_2(r_2)} = \frac{A}{K_2}\lambda. \tag{4.64}$$

If the values g_1, g_2, λ, and A/K_2 are specified, the rate of profit in the consumption goods sector, r_2, can be determined by the above. Eqs.(4.56), (4.57) can be transformed as follows.

$$g_1^{t+1} = g_1^t + \beta_1\left(\frac{g_1^t + g_2^t\lambda^t}{\sigma_1} - 1\right) \tag{4.65}$$

$$g_2^{t+1} = g_2^t + \beta_2\left\{\delta_2\left(g_1^t, g_2^t, \lambda^t, \frac{A^t}{K_2^t}\right) - 1\right\}. \tag{4.66}$$

In addition, we can obtain from (4.52)–(4.55),

$$\lambda^{t+1} = \frac{1 + g_2^t - d_2}{1 + g_1^t - d_1}\lambda^t. \tag{4.67}$$

And from Eqs.(4.52)–(4.55), (4.58), and (4.59), the equation below holds.

$$\frac{A^{t+1}}{K_2^{t+1}} = \frac{1+G_a}{1+g_2^t-d_2}\frac{A^t}{K_2^t} \tag{4.68}$$

$$\frac{L^{t+1}}{K_2^{t+1}} = \frac{1+G_n}{1+g_2^t-d_2}\frac{L^t}{K_2^t}. \tag{4.69}$$

The model of underemployment consists of four equations; (4.61)–(4.64). The equilibrium values of the model are:

$$g_1^* = G_a + d_1 \tag{4.70}$$

$$g_2^* = G_a + d_2 \tag{4.71}$$

$$\lambda^* = \frac{\sigma_1 - G_a - d_1}{G_a + d_2} \tag{4.72}$$

$$\left(\frac{A}{K_2}\right)^* = \sigma_2 - \frac{n_1\sigma_1/\lambda^* + n_2\sigma_2}{r_1^*/\sigma_2 R_1^* + n_2} \tag{4.73}$$

where

$$R_1^* = \frac{1 - r_1^*/\sigma_1}{n_1}.$$

The model will be switched from under-employment to full-employment when the value of $N_1 + N_2$ becomes larger than that of L.

(Constraint model)

[A] $N_1 + N_2 \geq L$:

Only the production of the capital goods sector can be realized and that of the consumption good sector will be constrained.

[B] $R_2 \leq R_{min}$:

The value of R is set at R_{min} and the basic consumption A will be reduced.

[C] $g_1, g_2 < 0$: $g_i = 0$

[D] $\delta_1 > \delta_{1max}$: $\delta_1 = \delta_{1max}$.

The rates of accumulation in both sectors will be reduced proportionately.

4.4.3 Programs

```
10 '**************************
20 ' One Sector Basic Model
30 '**************************
40 PERIOD=200
50 DIM G(PERIOD),AK(PERIOD),LK(PERIOD)
60 DIM DEL(PERIOD),R(PERIOD),PR(PERIOD)
70 DIM E(PERIOD)
80 '
90 '******* Parameter *******
100 SIG=.15
110 NC=1
120 BETA=.07
130 ES=.95
140 GN=.055
150 GA=.055
160 D=.005
170 PRS=.08
180 EPS=.45
190 '
200 '******* Equilibrium *******
210 GS=GA+D
220 AKS=PRS - GS
230 LKS=NC * SIG/ES
240 RS=(1 - PRS/SIG)/NC
250 '
260 RMIN=.01 * RS
270 DELMAX = ((1 - RMIN * NC) * SIG/PRS)^(EPS/(1 - EPS))
280 PRMAX=(1 - RMIN * NC) * SIG * DELMAX
290 '
300 '******* Initial Value *******
310 G0=.95 : AK0=1.15 : LK0=1.15
320 G(0)=G0 * GS
330 AK(0)=AK0 * AKS
340 LK(0)=LK0 * LKS
350 GOSUB 490
```

```
360 '
370 '********* Computation *******
380 PRINT "    T    g    A/K    L/K "
    ; "del    R    r    e"
390 FOR T=1 TO PERIOD
400 G(T)=G(T - 1)+BETA * (DEL(T - 1) - 1): IF G(T) <0
    THEN G(T)=0
410 AK(T)=AK(T - 1) * (1+GA)/(1+G(T - 1) - D)
420 LK(T)=LK(T - 1) * (1+GN)/(1+G(T - 1) - D)
430 GOSUB 490
440 PRINT USING "###";T;
450 PRINT USING "#.#####";G(T),AK(T),LK(T),DEL(T),
    R(T),PR(T),E(T)
460 NEXT T
470 END
480 '
490 PR(T)=G(T)+AK(T)
500 IF PR(0)=0 THEN DEL(T)=0 : R=1/NC : GOTO 600
510 DEL(T)=(PR(T)/PRS)^EPS
520 DELFULL=LK(T)/NC/SIG
530 IF DEL(T) <= DELMAX OR DELFULL < DELMAX
    THEN GOTO 580
540 R(T)=RMIN
550 DEL(T)=DELMAX
560 PR(T)=PRMAX
570 IF G(T) > PR(T) THEN G(T)=PR(T)
580 R(T)=(1 - PR(T)/SIG/DEL(T))/NC
590 '
600 IF DEL(T) < DELFULL THEN GOTO 700
610 '
620 DEL(T)=DELFULL
630 R(T)=(DEL(T) * SIG - G(T) - AK(T))/LK(T)
640 IF R(T) > RMIN THEN GOTO 680
650 R(T)=RMIN
660 IF G(T) < DEL(T) * SIG - R(T) * LK(T) THEN GOTO 680
670 G(T)=DEL(T) * SIG - R(T) * LK(T)
```

```
680 PR(T)=(1 - R(T) * NC) * DEL(T) * SIG
690 '
700 E(T)=DEL(T)/DELFULL
710 RETURN
```

```
10 '***************************
20 ' Two-sector Basic Model
30 '***************************
40 PERIOD=200
50 DIM G1(PERIOD),DEL1(PERIOD),PR1(PERIOD),R1(PERIOD)
60 DIM G2(PERIOD),DEL2(PERIOD),PR2(PERIOD),R2(PERIOD)
70 DIM LAM(PERIOD),LK(PERIOD),AK(PERIOD)
80 DIM E(PERIOD),G(PERIOD),PR(PERIOD)
90 '
100 '******* Parameter *******
110 SIG1=.75 : NC1=1 : BETA1=.007 : D1=.005
120 SIG2=.15 : NC2=1 : BETA2=.003 : D2=.005
130 PR1S=.08 : EPS1=.45
140 PR2S=.08 : EPS2=.45
150 ES=.95
160 GN=.055
170 GA=.055
180 '
190 '******* Equilibrium *******
200 G1S=GA+D1
210 G2S=GA+D2
220 LAMS=(SIG1 - G1S)/G2S
230 R1S=(1 - PR1S/SIG1)/NC1
240 R2S=R1S/(PR1S/SIG2+R1S * NC2)
250 NKS=NC1 * SIG1+NC2 * SIG2 * LAMS
260 LKS=NKS/ES
270 AKS=SIG2 - R2S * NKS/LAMS
280 '
290 R1MIN=.01 * R1S
300 DEL1MAX=((1 - R1MIN * NC1) * SIG1/PR1S)^(EPS1/(1 - EPS1))
310 R2MIN=.01 * R2S
320 '
330 '******* Initial Value *******
340 T=0 : G10=0! : G20=0! :LAM0=.03 : LK0=.1 : AK0=.1/.03
350 G1(0)=G1S * G10
360 G2(0)=G2S * G20
```

```
370 LAM(0)=LAMS * LAM0
380 LK(0)=LKS * LK0
390 AK(0)=AKS * AK0
400 GOSUB 560
410 '
420 '* * * * * * * Computation * * * * * * *
430 PRINT "time       g1 "; "g2       g"
440 FOR T=1 TO PERIOD
450 G1(T)=G1(T - 1)+BETA1 * (DEL1(T - 1) - 1) : IF G1(T)
    < 0 THEN G1(T)=0
460 G2(T)=G2(T - 1)+BETA2 * (DEL2(T - 1) - 1) : IF G2(T)
    < 0 THEN G2(T)=0
470 LAM(T)=LAM(T - 1) * (1+G2(T - 1) - D2)/(1+G1(T - 1) - D1)
480 LK(T)=LK(T - 1) * (1+GN)/(1+G1(T - 1) - D1)
490 AK(T)=AK(T - 1) * (1+GA)/(1+G2(T - 1) - D2)
500 GOSUB 560
510 PRINT T,G1(T),G2(T),G(T)
520 NEXT T
530 END
540 '
550 '* * * * * * * Capital goods sector * * * * * * *
560 DEL1(T)=(G1(T)+G2(T) * LAM(T))/SIG1
570 IF DEL1(T) <= DEL1MAX THEN GOTO 610
580 G1(T)=G1(T) * DEL1MAX/DEL1(T)
590 G2(T)=G2(T) * DEL1MAX/DEL1(T)
600 DEL1(T)=DEL1MAX
610 IF DEL1(T) > 0 THEN GOTO 650
620 PR1(T)=0
630 R1(T)=1/NC1
640 GOTO 690
650 PR1(T)=PR1S * DEL1(T)∧(1/EPS1)
660 R1(T)=(1 - PR1(T)/SIG1/DEL1(T))/NC1
670 '
680 '* * * * * * * Consumption goods sector * * * * * * *
690 SMIN=0 : SMAX= - 1 : PR2(T)=PR2S
700 DEL2(T)=(PR2(T)/PR2S)∧EPS2
```

```
710 SA=AK(T)/SIG2/DEL2(T)
720 IF ABS(SMAX - SMIN) < .000001 THEN GOTO 790
730 SF=(1 - SA) * PR2(T) - R1(T) * (NC1 * SIG1 * DEL1(T)/LAM(T)
    +NC2 * AK(T))
740 IF SMAX < 0 AND SF < 0
    THEN SMIN=PR2(T) : PR2(T)=PR2(T) * 2 : GOTO 700
750 IF SF < 0 THEN SMIN=PR2(T) : GOTO 770
760 SMAX=PR2(T)
770 PR2(T)=(SMAX+SMIN)/2 : GOTO 700
780 '
790 NK=NC1 * SIG1 * DEL1(T)+NC2 * SIG2 * DEL2(T) * LAM(T)
800 R2(T)=(SIG2 * DEL2(T) - AK(T)) * LAM(T)/NK
810 '
820 '* * * * * * * Full employment * * * * * * *
830 IF NK < LK(T) THEN GOTO 1040
840 '
850 '* * * * * * * Full employment:Computation * * * * * * *
860 NK=LK(T)
870 IF (1 - R2MIN * NC2) * LK(T) < NC1 * SIG1 * DEL1(T)
    THEN GOTO 930
880 DEL2(T)=(LK(T) - NC1 * SIG1 * DEL1(T))/(NC2 * SIG2 *
    LAM(T))
890 R2(T)=(SIG2 * DEL2(T) - AK(T)) * LAM(T)/LK(T)
900 IF R2(T) < R2MIN THEN R2(T)=R2MIN
910 GOTO 1020
920 '
930 R2(T)=R2MIN
940 DEL2(T)=R2(T) * LK(T)/(SIG2 * LAM(T))
950 SG=(LK(T) - NC2 * DEL2(T) * SIG2 * LAM(T))/(NC1 *
    SIG1 * DEL1(T))
960 DEL1(T)=DEL1(T) * SG
970 G1(T)=G1(T) * SG
980 G2(T)=G2(T) * SG
990 PR1(T)=PR1S * DEL1(T)∧(1/EPS1)
1000 R1(T)=(1 - PR1(T)/(SIG1 * DEL1(T)))/NC1
1010 '
```

```
1020 PR2(T)=(1 - R2(T) * NC2) * SIG2 * DEL2(T) * R1(T)/R2(T)
1030 '
1040 E(T)=NK/LK(T)
1050 G(T)=(G1(T)+G2(T) * LAM(T))/(1+LAM(T))
1060 PR(T)=(PR1(T)+PR2(T) * LAM(T))/(1+LAM(T))
1070 RETURN
```

Chapter 5

Metamorphosis of Business Cycle

5.1 Monopoly and the Metamorphoses

By the beginning of the twentieth century the major capitalistic countries of the world accomplished their transformation from competitive to monopolistic capitalism. The core areas of their economies were seized by a small number of giant firms. For example, in 1904 in the United States the big firms producing no less than one million dollars of annual output, which accounted for only 0.9 percent of the total 100,900 firms, employed 25.6 percent of workers and produced 38 percent of the total output. In Germany, the biggest 0.9 percent of firms employed 39.4 percent of workers, 75.3 percent of steam engines and 77.2 percent of electric power.[1]

We call this development of the capitalist system the monopolistic stage of capitalism. In this stage, private decisions, made by a small number of big firms, have serious effects on the whole economy. Let us consider, for example, the movement of prices. It was usual in the nineteenth century for prices to fall in a depression. However, by the twentieth century the situation has changed. Table 5.1 shows how prices and output were affected in the three years after the Great Depression of 1929.[2] It can be seen that, in competitive markets, such as the food and textile industries, prices decreased more than output, but in monopolistic markets such as the iron and steel industry and the automobile industry the result was the opposite, namely, the output decreased greatly and prices were maintained. These

[1]V.I. Lenin, *Imperialism, the Highest Stage of Capitalism*, Peking, Foreign Language Press,1965. Chapter 1.

[2]Source: U.S. National Resources Committee, *The Structure of the American Economy*, vol.1

Table 5.1 Prices and Outputs by Industries in the U.S., 1929-32, (the rate of fall (%))

		prices	*outputs*
1	Motor vehicles	12	74
2	Agricultural implements	14	84
3	Iron and Steel	16	76
4	Cement	16	55
5	Auto tires	25	42
6	Leather products	33	18
7	Petroleum products	36	17
8	Textile products	39	28
9	Food products	39	10
10	Agricultural commodities	54	1

facts seem to indicate the monopolistic power of giant firms to control prices. Thus we need to investigate concretely the microeconomic behavior of the giant monopolistic firms in order to analyse macroeconomic problems.

The development of the capitalist economy has inevitably been accompanied by an increase in the power of organized labour. In England, the membership of labour unions increased from two million to about eight million within the first twenty years of the twentieth century, and the percentage of unionized workers was raised from ten to thirty-five percent (*cf.* Figure 5.1).[3] This evolution brought about the general strike of 1926 which ended in vain and thereafter, confronting the great depression, the labour movement fell into a stagnant state. However, these experiences teach us that the organized power of worker has steadily progressed enough to fight a general strike for better wages, and it is damaging for capitalists to neglect the enhanced power of workers, and may even lead to a crisis of capitalism.

[3]Source: B.R.Mitchell & P.Deane, *Abstract of British Historical Statistics*, 1971

Figure 5.1 Labour Union Membership, 1892 to 1937 in U.K.
(in thousands)

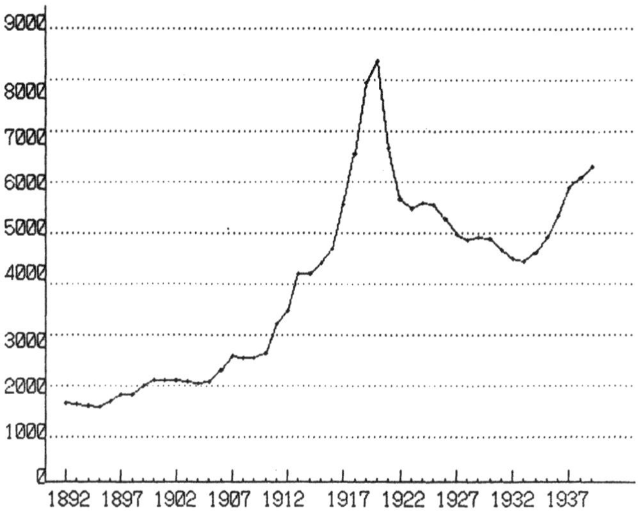

Figure 5.2 Labour Union Membership in non-agricultural establishments,
1930 to 1955 in U.S.A.
(in percentage)

Table 5.2 Government Spending (Percentage in GNP)

U.K.		U.S.A.		JAPAN	
1890	8.8	1890	7		
1900	14.4	1903	7		
1910	12.8	1913	7		
1920	26.1	1923	12	1920	17.6
1928	24.2	1929	12	1925	20.6
1933	25.9	1933	27	1930	28.4
1938	30.1			1935	31.7
		1940	22	1937	35.9
		1947	26	1941	50.7
1950	39.5	1950	25	1955	28.5
1955	37.3	1953	34	1960	27.1

In the United States, the number of organized workers at the start of the Great Depression was as low as 12 percent if we neglect farmers, but it has drastically increased throughout the 1930s and after the Second World War so that finally it amounted to 35.8 percent in 1945 (see Figure 5.2).[4]

The strength of workers' organization reveals itself not only in claims for higher wages but also in claims for various improvements of labour conditions like short working hours, unemployment allowances, public assurances of housing, medical care, public education and so on. Why government intervention has come to play such a large role in this century can be first understood by recognizing the increased claims for social welfare by the working class. The capitalist class must accept workers' demands, even unwillingly, in order to maintain their position as a ruling class in a capitalist society. Thus by the middle of twentieth century, the share of government spending in the total national output has increased to thirty to forty percent in almost all the main capitalist countries (see Table 5.2).[5]

---

[4]Source: U.S. Department of Commerce, *Historical Statistics of the United States*, 1960.

[5]Sources: T.Shima, *Theory of Public Finance (in Japanese)*, Iwanami 1963, pp.53-57. (U.K.: Peacock & Wiseman, *The Growth of Public Expenditure in U.K.*, U.S.A.: Shultz & Harris, *American Public Finance*, JAPAN: Y.Yamada, *Estimation of National Income in Japan (in Japanese)*)

In this chapter we examine the metamorphoses of the business cycle at the monopolistic stage of capitalism. We characterize this stage by:

- the dominance of a small number of giant firms,
- an increase in the strength of unionized workers,
- a big role for government intervention in the economy.

5.1.1 The Monopolistic Behavior of Firms and Workers

Decision of output and price

In a competitive economy firms can not control their selling prices. They can no choose but to passively accept the prevailing prices as given. The capital equipment which they own is either utilized at full capacity or is not utilized at all. If the prices assure even a low rate of profit, it is rational for the capitalists to utilize the equipment fully. How then is total output determined? A price increase brings about an increase in the number of firms operating at full capacity, and conversely, a fall in price compels profitable equipments to be shut down one by one. Thus the total output in the economy is determined by the selling price compared with the unit factor cost, *i.e.* the real wage rate in terms of selling prices. The overall utilization rate of equipment is the magnitude of actual output divided by the potential output capacity of existing capital equipment. Therefore, a rise in the real wage rate leads a fall in the capital utilization rate, δ, in the economy as a whole. From:

$$\delta = \delta(R) \qquad \delta' < 0 \tag{5.1}$$

and the definition of profit rate, r:

$$r = \delta\sigma(1 - Rn) \tag{5.2}$$

where n is the labour coefficient, and σ is the normal output-capital ratio, we have:

$$\delta_t = \delta(r_t) \tag{5.3}$$
$$1 = \delta(r^*) \quad \delta' > 0. \tag{5.4}$$

The utilization rate of the whole economy can be expressed as an increasing function of the profit rate, notwithstanding the fact that an individual firm either utilizes its capital equipment at full capacity or shuts it down completely.

Let us consider next monopolistic firms. They do not accept selling prices passively, but try to affect them in order to assure maximum profits by controlling output levels. They may even shut down less profitable machinery when they do not think the profits are satisfactory. A monopolistic capitalist has a required function concerning the profit rate. We assume here that the required profit rate is an increasing function of the utilization rate of their capital equipment,

$$r^* = r^*(\delta) \tag{5.5}$$

which is expressed exactly the same as the equation above. In this case, as distinct from a competitive economy, the function δ means the monopolistic behavior itself. The more profits the monopolistic firm requires the more the function δ shifts to the right.

The Investment Decision

The investment decision of a competitive firm is assumed to be:

$$g_{t+1} = g_t + \beta(\delta_t - 1), \quad \beta > 0. \tag{5.6}$$

The rate of accumulation, which is defined as the amount of investment divided by the total capital stock, is increased in the next period when the rate of utilization of capital equipment during the present period exceeds the normal level and vice versa. Here the rate of utilization in the present period is used as a proxy for capitalists' future expectations of market conditions. If capital equipment is normally utilized during the period t, they are assumed to expect future demand to increase at the same rate as period t, so that maintain the same rate of accumulation in the next period. In the case of over-utilization, they decide to raise the rate of accumulation because of the shortage of productive equipment.

There is no difference between a competitive economy and a monopolistic economy in the sense that decisions about investment are made separately by many capitalists relying on their own subjective expectations. The monopolistic firm's investment decision making, however, has some characteristics different from those of competitive firms.

- The monopolistic stage of capitalism is characterized by the overwhelming role of durable goods in production. The minimum necessary capital needed for standard production activities become huge and the durability of capital equipment is lengthened so that their decision making must rely more heavily on long-run expectations.

- The monopolistic firm can command adequate funds compared to the competitive firm. If necessary, from the point of view of long-run considerations, they can invest vast amounts of money even during a recession.

These circumstances mean that monopolistic firms' decisions are made from a long-run perspective and that current economic conditions have less influence in their thinking. This is expressed by the smaller value of β in the investment function above.

The Decision to Shutdown Capital Equipment

A competitive firm is forced to stop operating its equipment when it ceases to produce profits any more. In a recessionary phase of the business cycle, the prices in terms of nominal wages fall so that the real wage rate is raised, which compels the non-profitable machinery to be shut down. Even if capitalists expect a future rise in selling prices, they can not survive the recession due to their weak financial capacity. Thus, the capital depreciation rate, denoted by d, can be expressed as a function of the real wage rate R.

$$d_t = \Phi(R_t) \qquad \Phi' > 0 \tag{5.7}$$

Under the monopolistic stage, however, this forced shut down is weakened for the following reasons:

- Prices are sustained by monopolies in a recession, and so the rise of the real wage rate is weakened.
- They can endure recessions due to their strong financial power.
- On the other hand, they may shut down still profitable equipment because of their required profit rate function. This implies that the mutual relationship between the depreciation rate and the real wage rate is weakened in the monopolistic stage. This is expressed by a smaller value of Φ' in the function above.

Worker's Behavior to Realize its Objectives

Worker's behavior to realize its objectives is enhanced corresponding to firms' monopolistic behaviors. As criteria of the degree of workers' strength we can consider the followings:

1. an increase in the nominal wage rate
2. an increase in the real wage rate
3. an increase in the share of output distributed to workers.

If workers have no organized power to realize their objectives, the nominal wage rate will rise and fall according to the labour market conditions of supply and demand. The behavior (1) above surely implies a stronger position for labour than this. However, as the capitalists have the power to control prices, the benefit from an increase in nominal wage rate is squeezed out by inflation as long as workers are satisfied with only an increase in the nominal wage rate. In order for workers to assure an increase in real wages, they must raise their nominal wages in terms of prices. If they want to raise the share of output received by labour they must succeed in raising the real wage rate above the increase in labour productivity. But this is not enough.

Suppose workers succeed in raising the real wage rate. But as long as capitalists monopolistically control production decision making, they will lower the capital utilization rates because of low profit rates. This brings about an excess demand in the commodity market and prices inevitably go up. Thus the nominal wage increase does not lead to a real wage increase unless workers succeed in constraining the capitalists' production decision makings. This is, however, still not enough.

Suppose workers succeed in raising the real wage rate by successfully forcing capitalists produce under low profit rates. Even then, if the production decisions on investment are made solely by capitalists, potential output will be gradually decreased by the physical depreciation of the capital equipment. And ultimately, the increased real wage rate can not be sustained. Therefore, it is absolutely necessary for workers to participate in the decision making processes, not only concerning production, but also investment, in order to realize and maintain the increased real wage rate.

The monopolistic stage is established by the increased power of workers corresponding to (1). The important characteristics of this stage, however, are the class struggles relating to (2) and (3). However, workers' ability to realize (1) is, of course, the necessary condition for them to proceed to (2) and (3). Because it is impossible to raise either the real wage rate or the share output going to labour without having the power to raise the nominal wage rate. In this sense, (1) is a fundamental condition for labour to realize its objectives. In the light of this we express the wage function at this stage as:

$$W_{t+1} = W_t \left\{ 1 + \omega_1 \left(1 - \frac{R_t}{R^*} \right) + \omega_2 \left(\frac{N_t}{L_t} - e^* \right) \right\} \tag{5.8}$$

where R^* means the required real wage rate of workers. The second term in the parenthesis of the right hand side of the above equation implies that workers try to raise the nominal wage rate to realize their required level, denoted by R^*. The third term implies a labour market pressure such that higher employment than normal raises wages, where e^* means the natural rate of employment. In the competitive economy, the parameter value of ω_1 is small and that of ω_2 is large, and conversely, in the monopolistic economy,

ω_1 is large and ω_2 is small and R^* will be greater.

5.1.2 The Cumulative Property of the Disequilibrium Accumulation Process and Monopoly

In this section we examine how business cycles are metamorphosed by the changes in behavior of capitalists and workers described in the previous section. Towards that end, we take up the following problems in turn:

- The effects of monopolistic behaviors on the cumulative property of disequilibrium in the commodity market.
- The effects on the possibilities of downward economic reversals.
- The effects on the possibilities of upward economic reversals.

The Cumulative Mechanism of the Accumulation Process

Let us begin at the beginning. The cumulative property of the accumulation process can be summarized as: Suppose there exists an excess demand in the commodity market during the current period. The degree of disequilibrium in the next period depends on the mutual changes of supply and demand from the current to the next period. This gap grows period by period, because the increasing rate of supply in period t is mainly determined by the accumulation rate of capital in the period $t-1$, and, on the other hand, the increasing rate of demand in the period t is determined by the increasing rate of accumulation during the same period, which depends on the market condition in the period $t-1$ and the accumulation rate during the period $t-1$. In the upward process the accumulation rate of capital at period t is greater than that at period $t-1$ so that the discrepancy between supply and demand during period t is enlarged. This is the essence of the cumulative property of the accumulation process in the capitalistic economy.

There exist some other factors affecting this cumulative process, which we consider in turn. As to the factors affecting supply in the next period we have to consider a change in the capital utilization rate and a change in the capital depreciation rate, which may arise due to a change in the real wage rate. As to the factors affecting demand we have to consider changes in consumption demands. These factors will modify the cumulative process in the capitalistic economy, although they will not ultimately prevent it from occurring. The downwards cumulative process can be explained in the same manner. How is this cumulative property affected by monopolistic behaviors?

The Effects of Monopoly on the Cumulative Property of Business Cycles

The tendency towards a cumulative property during the upward phase of the cycle may be moderated by the monopolistic behaviors of big firms for the following reasons:

- The investment decisions of big firms depend strongly on the long-run and therefore much more unreliable expectations and thus the effects of current market conditions are weakened, which tends to suppress the increase in investment demand in the next period.

- The monopolistic firms' behaviors when they face excess demand is characterized more by a reliance on price increases and less on output increases, which will tend to suppress consumption demands in the next period.

- A further fall in the real wage rate, due to monopolistic pricing behavior, weakens the forced depreciation of capital equipment, which, in turn, raises the supply of capital goods in the next period.

On the other hand, the effects of monopoly are ambiguous on the cumulative process in the downward direction.

- The mitigating effects of the current excess supply on investment decisions moderates a fall in investment demand in the next period.

- The monopolistic pricing behaviors tend to accelerate the decrease in consumption demand due to its effects on both employment and the real wage rate, which will bring about a large reduction of aggregate demand in the next period.

- The suppressing of increases in the real wage rate, by monopolistic pricing behavior, weakens the forced depreciation of capital in a downward process, which enables unprofitable equipment to survive longer and further exacerbates the condition of excess supply in the next period.

The first factor moderates the disequilibrium situation in the next period but the other two factors accelerate it. We can not say, a priori, which factor is stronger. It is interesting, however, to note that monopolistic decisions on capital utilization rates may act as an accelerator of disequilibrium even if it is thought by individual capitalists to assure their monopolistic prices and profits. This implies that even a giant firm can not control simultaneously both the output sold and the price at which it is sold, which are the two fundamental characteristics of the commodity producing economy.

In summary, the monopolistic behaviors mitigate the cumulative property in the upward direction. They moderate it in the downward process when the effect of a change in investment behavior dominates the effect of a change in the utilization decision, and, conversely, they accelerate it when the opposite is the case.

5.1.3 A Downwards Turn of the Business Cycle and Monopoly

The cumulative property of the upward accumulation process is mitigated by monopolistic behavior. How then is the duration of this boom process, from its beginning to its reversal into the downward process, affected? As we can not specify a particular occasion for this reversal, a priori, so we examine some probable opportunities for reversal, and consider how monopolistic behaviors affect the duration of the upward process. The following factors are considered to prolong the whole upward process:

- A mitigation of the cumulative property of capital accumulation process.

- A postponement of bottlenecks.

The mitigation of cumulative process accompanies a slow down in the increase in labour demand. The labour supply, which is exogenously given, forms the ceiling of the upward phase of the business cycle. The duration of which is prolonged when the growth in labour demand is moderated. The reasons are as follows: The rate of capital utilization, along this labour supply ceiling, is determined jointly by two increasing rates, the rate of labour supply and the rate of increase in the capital stock. The rate of increase in the capital stock is obviously greater than that of labour supply when the economy reaches the ceiling. Thus the capital utilization rate is gradually decreased until finally it becomes lower than the normal level, after which the rate of capital accumulation begins to fall, which accompanies a fall in the rate of labour demand. When at last labour demand becomes less than labour supply, the economy departs from the ceiling. Thus we can conclude that the whole upward, labour constrained, process is prolonged by the moderation of capital accumulation behavior.

A slow down of capital accumulation weakens not only labour demand but also the increasing rates of demand for raw materials, energy, land and so on. This means that the whole process is also prolonged for these additional reasons.

There are several kinds of bottlenecks in the upward process, such as labour supply, raw materials, energy, land availability and so on, each of which may be a possible opportunity for the reversal of the process. To break through these bottlenecks, capitalists try to purchase labour from other sectors, import materials from abroad, assure overseas energy supplies and so on. Moreover they try to develop and introduce new technologies which avoid or overcome these bottlenecks. To these ends, they offer higher wages or higher material prices and invest a vast amount in research and development, which only the monopolistic capitalists can afford. Further, they are able to exercise control over many affiliated firms and even make use of government power to achieve their private ends. Monopolistic firms retain strong connections with financial intermediaries. As a result they stand on a firmer financial bases compared with competitive firms, which is an advantageous condition for the continuation of the upward process. On the other hand, the followings factors may shorten this process:

- A stagnant condition of non monopolistic and competitive firms.
- A strong movement of workers to realize their demands.

Monopolistic prices in the producer goods sector lower the profit rates in non-monopolistic and consumer goods sectors. The control of supply by monopolistic firms and the resulting fall in the real wage rate reduce the income of wage earners, which leads to a fall in consumption demand and a fall in capital utilization and in profit rates in the consumer goods sectors. If it brings about a general decrease in accumulation demand of the whole economy, a reversal of the upward cumulative process into a downwards process happens. This possibility is strengthened due to the economic distress of the non-monopolistic and consumer goods sectors. In the upward process, the labour market as well as the goods market is in excess demand, which brings about higher wages and prices. When workers claim an increase in labour's share of the output, this wage-price spiral is much accelerated. Under conditions of accelerating inflation capitalists may experience difficulty in forming reliable long run expectations, which will result in a fall of accumulation demand. Thus the possibility of an early reversal of the upwards business cycle will be strengthened.

In summary, the consequences of monopolistic behavior on the duration of the upward cumulative process are contradictory. If worker's strength is not developed, monopolistic firms can realize their demands without provoking inflation spirals. Then non-monopolistic firms can transfer the cost burdens of monopoly prices onto workers. In this case the shortening effects, described above, are moderated so that the upward process may last longer.

On the other hand, if worker is strong enough to accomplish its ends, capitalists are compelled to raise prices again and again to maintain their objectives. Then non-monopolistic firms will suffer losses from both wage increases and monopoly prices. In this case, the shortening effects described above will come into play and lead to an earlier reversal of the upward process into a downward process. Therefore, we conclude that the state of the class struggle between workers and capitalists affects the duration of the upward process. When labour is weak, capital can enjoy a long lasting upward process through the sacrifices of workers. When workers become strong, the opposite is the case because of the difficulty of shifting burdens onto the working class.

It is not correct to conclude from the above that workers' power always aggravates economic conditions. It is possible to realize balanced growth if labour is strong enough to control even monopolistic firms' decision making on investment and output. But that would be a completely different economy than ours. In the situation where workers are strong enough to raise wages but not so strong as to exert control over monopolistic firms, then the above statement is an inevitable conclusion. In this sense the economic aggravation due to worker's power happens because workers are strong in a one sense, but weak in another.

5.1.4 The Upwards Turn of the Business Cycle and Monopoly

As long as the capitalistic economy is maintained, the downwards cumulative path must be reversed by some reason and transformed into an upward path. How is this process affected by monopolistic behavior? To state our conclusions first, it is conceivable that monopolistic behaviors prolong the duration of the whole process from the beginning of downwards process to the reversal into an upwards process. The main reasons are:

1. A mitigation of accumulation demand.
2. A weakening of the forced scrapping of capital equipment.
3. A rise in the required rate of profit.
4. Straitened circumstances in the non-monopolistic and consumer goods sectors.
5. The weakening of the forced introduction of new technology.

The weaker responses of monopolistic capitalists, as compared to competitive capitalists, when facing excess demand in the market mitigates the cumulative character of the accumulation process in both the downwards and upwards directions, as already stated. This means that the duration of the downwards phase of the cycle is prolonged. That is, the process culminating in zero gross investment is slowed.

The real wage rate is raised in a downwards process. However, monopoly prices weaken this rise. As the result, the forced scrapping of capital equipment becomes weak and idle capacities still persist without being scrapped. For example, consider the bottom of business cycle where only capitalists' consumption demand sustains the economy. As time passes, the utilization rate of capital gradually rises due to the physical depreciation of capital equipment, and finally, when the utilization rate exceeds the normal level, investment demands begins again and an economic reversal happens. If this scrapping effect is weakened due to monopoly behavior, the whole process is prolonged.

Monopolistic firms demand higher profit rates, relative to competitive firms, in order to utilize their capital equipment at the normal level. This implies that the rate of profit which is needed to restore investment demand is higher. Therefore, the duration of periods which is required for the profit rate to recover to that higher level through capital depreciation must be longer.

Moreover, a rise of the required profit rate by monopolistic capitals tends to raise the possibility of the economy falling into the downwards process. To put it differently, the greater the warranted rates of growth become, the greater the possibility that the actual growth rates are below the warranted rates and then a downwards process ensues. A fall in the price of producer goods and its favourable effects on the consumer goods sectors may be an opportunity for economic recovery. This possibility is also weakened by monopolistic pricing behaviors. The constraining effects on consumption demand of monopoly prices may also weaken an economic recovery lead by the consumer goods sectors.

Competitive firms are forced to choose between suffering losses to the point of bankruptcy or introducing superior technologies. It may happen that the massive investments necessary for introducing new technologies create an upwards turning point in the economy. At the monopolistic stage of capitalism, however, this is a pressure only for non-monopolistic firms, and it does not work for monopolistic firms because they stand outside the compulsory competition in introducing technical innovations. In this way, the forced introduction of new technologies, which can reverse a downward phase of the business cycle, is considerably weakened by the existence of monopoly capitalism.

We must add some additional qualifications to these comments. As was already stated, monopolistic decision making concerning capital equipment utilization accelerates the downward cumulative process. But it does not necessarily mean that the duration of the recession as a whole is shortened, because this utilization behavior accompanies a rise in the required profit rate and a resulting fall in the real wage rate, which will tend to prolong the process due to the last four of the five factors discussed above. The actual outcome depends on the particular circumstances of each situation. But in contrast to the ambiguities involving utilization decisions, accumulation decisions, in the monopoly environment, will always tend to prolong the downwards process.

What is the effect of strong labour organization? The monopolistic behaviors accelerate a reduction of employment, check a rising real wage rate and thus accelerate a reduction of workers' income in the downwards process. On the contrary, a successful labour campaign to constrain the monopolistic firms' behavior is thought to contribute to the support of aggregate demand, by raising consumption demand, which seems to mitigate the downward cumulative process. However, this does not necessarily mean that the downward process is shortened. Because if the capitalists' future expectations are aggravated by the antagonistic struggles of labour, this process may be prolonged by stagnant investment demand. Therefore, as long as the decision making on investment is held by capitalists, any partially successful movement of workers to challenge capitalists' power will worsen the economy and prolonging the downwards process.

In summary, at the monopolistic stage of capitalism the cumulative property of the accumulation process is moderated and the duration of both booms and recessions may be prolonged with some qualifications. We show the metamorphoses of business cycles using numerical simulations in Figure 5.3. The complete model and details of the numerical analysis are in the Appendix.

Figure 5.3 the Metamorphoses of business cycle by monopoly[6]

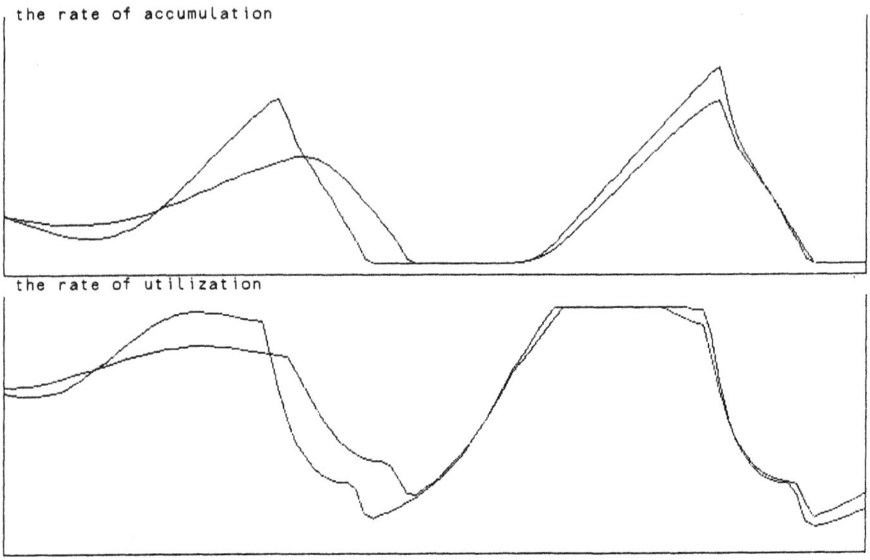

[6]First we compute using the parameters specified in the program (see below). Next we compute again, under the same initial condition, using different parameters, *i.e.* to reduce the values of β, d_1, ω_2 by 10% and to raise that of $r^*, \epsilon_1, \omega_1$ by 10%.

5.2 Government Intervention and the Metamorphoses

5.2.1 The Necessity of Government Intervention

We have shown that, at the monopolistic stage of the capitalist economy, business cycles are modified and both boom and recession are likely to be prolonged. This injures the stability of the capitalistic economy and makes government intervention into the economy inevitable for a number of reasons. A prolonged recession means a persistent realization crisis. The rate of profit and the capital utilization rate remain low for a long period and workers suffer severe unemployment problems. It becomes unendurable for both workers and capitalists, especially for non-monopolistic capitalists, to endure the persistent recession and wait until an autonomous recovery. Organized labour feels a need to reform capitalism, which has long failed to control the economy and to supply employment opportunities, and then proceeds to act on this feeling, which undermines the political foundations of capitalism.

A prolonged boom needs the continual provision of infrastructure to maintain the conditions for a growing economy, *i.e.* to assure that social capital investments like roads, harbours, water facilities, to replenish industrial mineral and energy resources and to treat public nuisances and environmental problems. These are tasks beyond the private firms' financial ability or are problems long neglected by private interests. Thus public funds and the government intervention based on public authority are needed to cope with these problems. When a country has a deficiency in the energy and material base, foreign and military policy to secure stable overseas bases is indispensable. Capitalists' behavior to gain monopolistic profits and workers' behavior to realize their objectives bring about hyper-inflation. Inflation affects people differently. Especially the most vulnerable sections of the population like the unemployed and pensioners are most harmed by inflation. Inflation may injure the competitiveness of the domestic economy, damage the trade balance and may bring about an economic recession. Accelerating inflation makes it difficult for capitalists to form future expectations and may bring about a decrease in accumulation demand. Therefore, in order to avoid these problems, government intervention is needed.

The government introduces an aggregate demand policy to cope with these problems. In a long lasting recession government spending is increased and other financial policies are employed to induce private demand. In an over-heating boon the opposite policies are introduced. Thus government aggregate demand policy can be considered a measure to avoid difficulties by reversing the upwards and downwards cumulative processes by stabilizing and limiting a trade cycle within a narrow range. If such a policy is effectively conducted, what new characteristics does it bring about? This is the next problem to be examined.

5.2.2 Monopoly and Aggregate Demand Policy

What is the condition for the aggregate demand policy to be effective? To examine this let us consider the economic mechanism of aggregate demand policy when it works best. Suppose an economy in recession. This policy works through the following three steps:

1. The fiscal demand raises total demand in the economy as a whole.

2. A rise in total demand raises output and employment.

3. A rise in output stimulates the capitalists' accumulation demand.

We examine how these steps are affected by monopolistic behaviors. It is not so obvious that fiscal policy succeeds in raising the aggregate demand as a whole. It may even happen that total demand decreases, not withstanding an increased fiscal demand, due to a decrease in other demand items. If the actual increase in total demand provoked by a fiscal policy stimulus is weaker than expected, it needs much more government spending in order to realize the initial policy purposes. Of the factors producing these problems, the two most important are the problems related to the targets of government spending and the methods of financing the spending.

First if government activity competes with private firms' activities, the government economic intervention may undermine the profitable conditions for private capitalists. Therefore the fields to which the government activities are directed are confined to public education, official affairs and the specific tasks relating to the construction of social overhead like railways, roads and industrial water facilities and other bonuses to alleviate private firms' burdens. These activities are indispensable for the capitalist class, but are beyond the individual capitalists' financial abilities. The fields competing with private firms are carefully avoided and the activities which were originally funded by public sources, once firmly established, can be privatised.

Corresponding to the increased role of government, bribes and briberies relating government funds become everyday affairs. The large amount of government spending is associated with the risk of militarization. As to the financial sources, government spending can only be financed through tax revenues, issuing bonds and printing money. A tax increase reduces disposable income and thus consumption demands, which offsets the stimulating effect of government spending. This effect is strong if the tax is levied against low income groups with a high propensity to consume, *i.e.* workers, it is best to levy the tax against high income groups, *i.e.* capitalists, in order to maximize the stimulating effects of government spending. However the method levying a tax in capitalist society is the inimical to this.

When the fund is raised by taxing workers, consumption demand is restrained and the government needs more funds to realize the demand increase initially intended. This will provoke resistance movements from the workers' side. Deficit spending must be financed by issuing bonds. An accumulation of bonds which is held by the private sector may lead to a fall in prices in the bond market and an increase in the rate of bond return. Thus by continuing deficit spending, the condition for issuing additional bonds is undermined. An increase in the rate of return of government bond brings about an overall increase in various kinds of interest rates including the lending rate of interest. This may injure the private investments, *i.e.* so called crowding-out effects. Thus it gradually becomes harder to continue deficit spending by issuing bonds.

If the central bank intervenes in the bond market to buy bonds while the government finances the deficit by issuing bonds, the situation is the same as if the deficit was financed directly by central bank printing money, thus being able to avoid negative effects of issuing bonds for the time being. For this to be practised the gold standard system, which connects the money supply to the gold stock, must be abandoned and the inconvertible currency system to be introduced. However an increase in the money supply brings about another problem: inflation.

Thus, aggregate demand policy, depending on deficit financing by issuing bonds or printing money, has its limits. To manage these limitations the capitalists try to introduce a new tax system which puts the onus on labour and an incomes policy which aims to cut wages, both of which are matters in vigorous current dispute.

Suppose that an aggregate demand is increased due to fiscal expansion. Can we expect an increase in output and employment? Denoting the aggregate nominal demand in terms of the nominal wage by D_w, and aggregate employment by N, the equilibrium condition of goods market is expressed as:

$$D_w = \phi(N) \tag{5.9}$$

where ϕ is the required proceeds of capitalists in terms of the wage rate, namely it expresses the capitalists' attitude about required profits. The price control exercised by monopolies, for example, shifts the function, ϕ, upwards. If this is the case, an increase in employment originated by fiscal expansion is limited and a bigger part of the nominal demand increase is absorbed by inflation.

Moreover we must note that a demand increase does not necessarily raise domestic employment. Monopolistic firms' activities at present extend to all over the world and their production, employment and sales are managed from a global viewpoint. Therefore a domestic demand increase in a particular country does not necessarily result in an increase in domestic output and employment. If it is profitable to produce abroad and import the completed goods, they will not hesitate to do so. As workers become strong, it becomes more and more profitable for capitalists to transfer their production bases abroad seeking manageable and cheap workers, cheap raw materials and low taxation. This is the countervailing effect to expansionary fiscal policy.

Suppose that the domestic production and employment are fortunately increased. However, unless they provoke an increase in private accumulation demands, an autonomous upwards process does not start and then the demand policy fails. Competitive firms always utilize their equipments around normal levels. Monopolistic capitals, however, have every reasons to utilize their capitals at levels below normal, especially in a recession the rate of capital utilization is lowered for the purpose of price control. Therefore, in order to raise the utilization rates up to normal, which is necessary for starting autonomous investment demands, the amount of fiscal increase must be greater in the monopolistic economy compared with the competitive economy.

Moreover the monopolistic firms' decision making on investment strongly depends on long-run expectations. Thus the government must practise a continuous fiscal expansion to improve their expectations. To convert the direction of investments from abroad to home, a conservative government will grant heavy subsidies or reduce taxes in favour of those capitals deciding on domestic investments. These policies put a heavy burden on the government.

To summarise, for fiscal policy to be effective it needs to activate the private activity, especially investment demand. However, this becomes harder to accomplish when monopoly capital prevails in the economy. The fact that the cumulative property is mitigated in monopolistic economy does not necessarily mean that government intervention is able to easily control private economic activity, but it must be strongly and continuously practiced to successfully manage the economy. If the intervention is weak, a recession is prolonged although it is not deep due to government activities. The difficulty in reversing the direction of the economy necessitates vast quantities of fiscal burdens undertaken for long periods. In this sense, a budget crisis is a product of monopolistic capitalism.

5.2.3 Stagflation

Stagflation is the phenomena of the simultaneous coexistence of inflation and stagnation. In a competitive market a boom will accompany a price increase, and vice versa. In this sense stagflation is a phenomena specific to the monopolistic economy. The cause of stagflation has been examined by many economists. We think the following conditions are important for that phenomena to arise:

1. An incompatibility of demands between capitalists and workers.
2. Workers realise their desire to raise nominal wages and capitalists their desire to raise their selling prices.

These conditions bring about a wage-price spiral even in a recession. In figure 5.4 the rate of capital utilization labelled B corresponds to the stationary state of prices, that is a balanced point where inflationary pressure due to raising wages and prices and a deflationary pressure due to excess supply in both the labour and goods markets are just equilibrating each other. We should note that the point B is below the normal utilization rate, indicated by A, because both capitalists and workers are strong enough to raise prices and wages even under a pressure of idle capacities and unemployment. Thus we have inflation even if the utilization rate is below normal. On the other hand, the rate of accumulation and therefore the growth rate of the economy will rise and fall according to whether the capital utilization rate is above or below the normal level. Therefore the point A is the critical point whether the economy moves upwards or downwards.

Figure 5.4 Stagflation

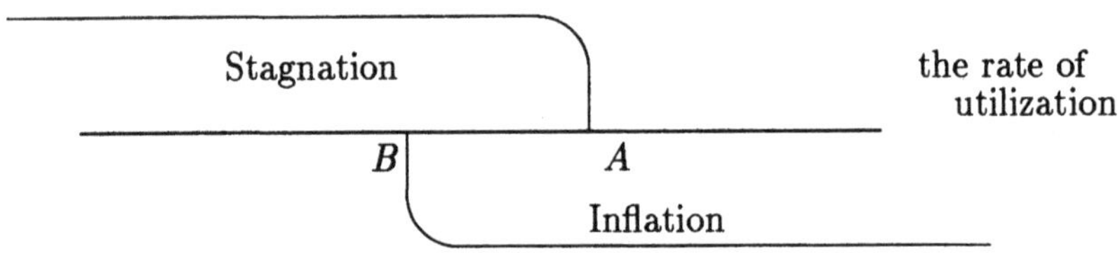

We have stagflation in the area between A and B. Such a phenomenon, however, has a temporary property unless the government intervenes into the economy. Because, however strong capitals are, they can not up hold their prices under the pressure of a severe depression. Similarly, even a strong labour organization will not be able to continue to raise wages if facing a vast number of unemployed.

Government intervention to stabilize the economy within a small range has played a role in establishing stagflation in the economy. A severe depression which might have pushed down prices is avoided by expanding government spending and thus the condition of the coexistence of inflation and recession is maintained by policy instruments. On the other hand, in the boom part of the business cycle the government deliberately introduces deflationary policies to get prevent hyper-inflation. As a result of these "stop and go policies" the stagflation phenomena has become a long continuing phenomena which is deeply embedded in the economy, and, at the same time, the amplitude and the periodic time of the business cycle are modified so that shallow and short-lived business cycles prevail accompanied by inflation throughout the cycle. Policy intervention under stagflation brings about increasing budget pressure on the government. Thus a budget crisis has a chronic character.

Figure 5.5 the Metamorphoses of Business Cycle
by Government Intervention[7]

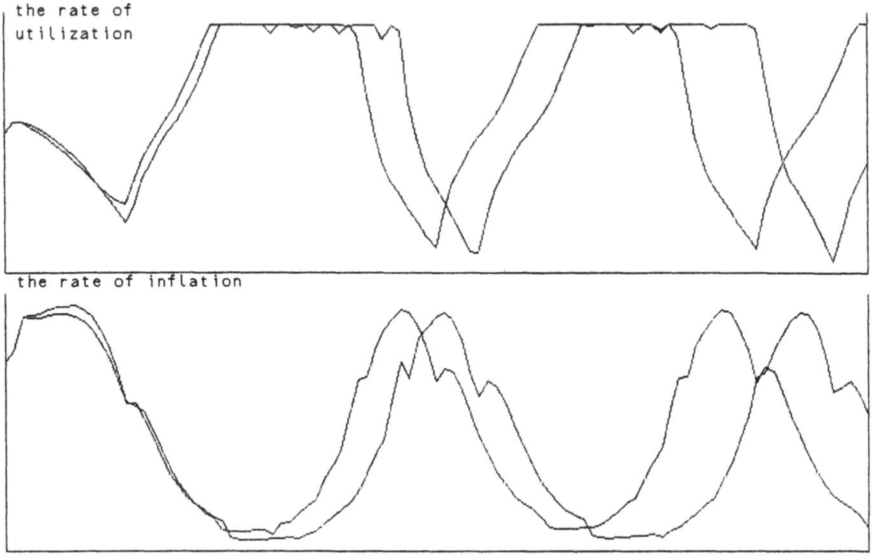

[7]First we compute using the parameters specified in the program. After that, we compute again under the same initial condition but the value of γ_1, γ_2 are raised by 20%.

5.2.4 Workers and the Business Cycle

The business cycle most clearly shows the disequilibrium and absurd properties of capitalism. In the upward process an over accumulation, a fall in real wage rate and an accumulation of backlogs occur, and in a downward process an idle capacity and unemployment accumulate. The business cycle is a continuum of both of these disequilibrium phenomena. These phenomena stem from the very structure capitalism. In a monopolistic economy the business cycle does not disappear but is modified. The amplitude of cycles becomes shallower and the duration of disequilibrium in both directions is prolonged. This implies a long continuing distress, not only for workers, but also for non-monopolistic capitalists. Thus it becomes difficult to leave the economy to autonomous recovery. Therefore, capitalism must rely on government intervention in order to avoid social and political conflicts. Government intervention results in a new phenomena called stagflation and a budget crisis is established as a permanent feature of the economy. This is a brief summary of this chapter. The role of business cycle is two-fold. First, a business cycle settles temporarily the difficulties produced in the course of the disequilibrium and cumulative accumulation process and creates the conditions for another period economic growth. Second, the productive forces of the economy are necessarily increased under the competitive pressures of the business cycle. It creates the physical and subjective foundations for a new society to be built after capitalism. Business cycles also will create many human beings who realise the fatal defects of capitalism and the necessity to reform it and have desires and abilities to act towards that end.

The former is a sustaining effect of capitalism, *i.e.* a negative feedback mechanism,(negative feedback mechanisms are ones which tend to maintain existing states and positive feedback causes systems to go out of control) and the latter is a transforming effect of capitalism, *i.e.* a positive feedback mechanism. Without business cycles capitalism can not survive and with business cycles capitalism will inevitably create the conditions to transform itself into a new society.

At the monopolistic stage the negative feedback mechanism is weakened in the sense that it needs to be supplemented by the government intervention. An economic system is stable if it is maintained by the market mechanism only. But if a system is maintained only with the support of the government, then the basis of that society becomes weak. The positive feedback mechanism of capitalism, *i.e.* the transforming effect of capitalism, is matured at the monopolistic stage. A monopoly is characterized by highly developed production technologies and rapid and massive data processing technologies. These are substantial material preconditions for a new society. Well educated, highly talented workers are also produced in large quantities under monopoly capital. Workers who possess enough knowledge and ability to make every decision about production. This implies that the subjective conditions for a new society have been achieved. Such a movement is accelerated by the possibility for the workers to organize a united front of peoples including farmers and non-monopolistic capitalists, who have common interests in the battle against monopolistic capitals.

At the monopolistic stage of capitalism, in order to maintain the exclusion of workers from fundamental decision making, the government needs a delicate ideology control, a conciliatory policy to the upper part of labour unions and to foster a right wing movement inside the parties of workers. These attempts, however, retard the progress of the society by perpetuating economic distress and producing a social and moral disintegration. For the majority in the society to improve their living conditions it is necessary to constrain monopolies and to put the decision making in the hands of the majority of people including workers. For this permanent and fundamental reform of the society, gradual and partial reforms are especially important. By experiencing many tiny and detailed activities for small improvements, workers are gradually trained to acquire a higher ability to organize more people and actually realise still broader and more fundamental reforms of capitalism. Through these trial and error experiences they are educated to know where key problems lie and the conditions needed for realizing their objectives. Some objectives are possible to fulfill even within capitalist society and other objectives must await a new society for their realization. To accomplish all their objectives they must finally grasp the governmental authority in their own hands. The business cycle is a school which educates workers to the necessity of doing so.

5.3 Mathematical Appendix

5.3.1 Monopoly Model

(Notations)

r^*: required rate of profit
δ^+: the upper limit of capital utilization rate
R^*: the required real wage rate of workers
e^*: the normal rate of employment
ν: the rate of increase of labour supply
R_{min}: the lower limit of real wage rate
ω_1, ω_2: parameters in wage function determined by workers
d_0, d_1: parameters in capital depreciation

(Model)
the equilibrium condition in commodity market

$$X_t = R_t N_t + I_t + A_t \tag{5.10}$$

a definition of capital utilization rate

$$X_t = \delta_t \sigma K_t \tag{5.11}$$

the determination of capital utilization rate

$$\delta_t = \left(\frac{r_t}{r^*}\right)^\epsilon, \quad 0 < \epsilon < 1 \tag{5.12}$$

a definition of profit rate

$$r_t = \frac{X_t - R_t N_t}{K_t} \tag{5.13}$$

investment function

$$g_{t+1} = g_t + \beta(\delta_t - 1), \quad \beta > 0 \tag{5.14}$$

a definition of capital accumulation rate

$$g_t = \frac{I_t}{K_t} \tag{5.15}$$

determination of employment

$$N_t = nX_t \tag{5.16}$$

determination of capital stock

$$K_{t+1} = K_t + I_t - d_t K_t \tag{5.17}$$

capital depreciation function

$$d_t = d_0 + d_1 R_t, \quad d_0 > 0 \quad d_1 > 0 \tag{5.18}$$

wage function

$$W_{t+1} = W_t \left\{ 1 + \omega_1 \left(1 - \frac{R_t}{R^*} \right) + \omega_2 \left(\frac{N_t}{L_t} - e^* \right) \right\} \tag{5.19}$$
$$\omega_1, \omega_2 > 0, \quad 0 < e^* < 1$$

labour supply

$$L_{t+1} = (1 + \nu) L_t \tag{5.20}$$

autonomous consumption

$$A_{t+1} = (1 + G_a) A_t \tag{5.21}$$

a definition of real wage rate

$$R_t = \frac{W_t}{P_t} \tag{5.22}$$

Constraints

[A]	$\delta \leq \delta^+$
[B]	$g \geq 0$
[C]	$N \leq L$
[D]	$R \geq R_{min}$

(Variables)
endogenous variables:

$X, I, K, A, N, L, R, P, W, \delta, g, r, d$

exogenous variables:

$\sigma, r^*, \epsilon, \beta, n, d_0, d_1, \omega_1, \omega_2, R^*, e^*, \nu, G_a, \delta^+, R_{min}$

The capital utilization function fulfills the properties that
(i) if r equals r^*, δ becomes zero
(ii) δ is an increasing function of r and
(iii)if r equals r^*, δ is exactly at normal level, *i.e.*, δ is unity.
Dividing both side of (5.10) by K and considering (5.13) and (5.15), we have

$$r_t = g_t = \frac{A_t}{K_t}. \tag{5.23}$$

Substituting (5.11) and (5.16) into (5.13) and by re-arranging it as to R, we have

$$R_t = \frac{1}{n}\left(1 - \frac{r_t}{\sigma\delta_t}\right). \tag{5.24}$$

Again substituting (5.11) into (5.16) and dividing it by K_t, we have

$$\frac{N_t}{K_t} = n\sigma\delta_t. \tag{5.25}$$

From (5.15), (5.17) and (5.21)

$$\frac{A_{t+1}}{K_{t+1}} = \frac{A_t}{K_t}\frac{1+G_a}{1+g_t-d_t} \tag{5.26}$$

From (5.15), (5.17) and (5.20),

$$\frac{L_{t+1}}{K_{t+1}} = \frac{L_t}{K_t}\frac{1+\nu}{1+g_t-d_t}. \tag{5.27}$$

Finally we can rewrite e_t as

$$e_t = \frac{N_t/K_t}{L_t/K_t} = \frac{n\sigma\delta_t}{L_t/K_t}. \tag{5.28}$$

Therefore (5.19) is rewritten as

$$W_{t+1} = W_t\left\{1+\omega_1\left(1-\frac{R_t}{R^*}\right)+\omega_2\left(e_t-e^*\right)\right\}. \tag{5.29}$$

Thus the reduced equations are composed by (5.23), (5.12), (5.24), (5.25), (5.18), (5.28), (5.29),(5.14),(5.26) and (5.27).
When the economy comes to violate the inequalities constraints from [A] to [D], we assume the followings according to each constraint.

Case A: When δ is greater than δ^+, we set δ as δ^+. Then the three items of demand,*i.e.* the workers' consumption, investment and the autonomous consumption, are impossible to be met simultaneously. We assume the the investment demand and the autonomous demand are realized, but the workers' consumption demand is cut to meet the total output. However, if this quota rule violates the real wage constraint [D], we assume that both investment and autonomous consumption are reduced proportionately in order to meet the minimum real wage rate.

Case B: If g becomes negative, we let g zero.

Case C: If N is greater than L, the utilization rate δ is restrained to meet the condition of $N = L$. Then the quota problem like the case [A] arises again. We assume the same quota rule relating three demand items.

Case D: If R is smaller than R_{min}, we set R as R_{min}. Then the utilization rate δ does not satisfy eq.(5.12) but is determined to fulfill the realization of R_{min}. In other words the capitalists are forced to raise the utilization rate. If this is impossible due to the technical upper bound δ^+, we assume that the investment and autonomous consumption are both proportionately reduced.

5.3.2 Government Intervention Model

(Notations)
F: Government Expenditure
t: the tax rate
r': the rate of profit after taxes
Z: budget deficit
i: the rate of interest
π: the rate of inflation
π^*: the policy goal,the rate of inflation
θ: rate of dependence of the budget deficit on government bond issues
ΔM: the Bond bought by central bank
r^*: the reference rate of profit in determination of the rate of utilization
r^{**}: the reference rate of profit in determination of investment
γ_1, γ_2: reaction parameters in government expenditure determination

(Model)
the equilibrium condition in commodity market

$$X_t = R_t N_t (1-t) + I_t + F_t \tag{5.30}$$

a definition of capital utilization rate

$$X_t = \delta_t \sigma K_t \tag{5.31}$$

the determination of capital utilization rate

$$\delta_t = \left(\frac{r_t}{r^*}\right)^{\epsilon}, \quad 0 < \epsilon < 1 \tag{5.32}$$

a definition of profit rate after taxes

$$r'_t = \frac{(X_t - R_t N_t)(1-t)}{K_t} \tag{5.33}$$

investment function

$$g_{t+1} = g_t + \beta_1(\delta_t - 1) + \beta_2(r'_{t+1} - i_{t+1} - r^{**}), \quad \beta_1, \quad \beta_2 > 0 \tag{5.34}$$

a definition of capital accumulation rate

$$g_t = \frac{I_t}{K_t} \tag{5.35}$$

determination of government expenditure

$$\frac{F_{t+1}}{K_{t+1}} = \frac{F_t}{K_t} + \gamma_1(1 - \delta_t) + \gamma_2(\pi^* - \pi_t) \tag{5.36}$$

budget constraint of government

$$A_t = tX_t + Z_t \tag{5.37}$$

determination of the rate of interest

$$\theta Z_t - \Delta M = B(X_t, i_t, r'_t) \tag{5.38}$$

determination of employment

$$N_t = nX_t \tag{5.39}$$

determination of capital stock

$$K_{t+1} = K_t + I_t - d_t K_t \tag{5.40}$$

capital depreciation function

$$d_t = d_0 + d_1 R_t, \quad d_0 > 0 \quad d_1 > 0 \tag{5.41}$$

wage function

$$W_{t+1} = W_t \left\{ 1 + \omega_1 \left(1 - \frac{R_t}{R^*} \right) + \omega_2 \left(\frac{N_t}{L_t} - e^* \right) \right\}, \omega_1, \omega_2 > 0, \quad 0 < e^* < 1 \tag{5.42}$$

labour supply

$$L_{t+1} = (1 + \nu) L_t \tag{5.43}$$

a definition of the rate of inflation

$$\pi_t = \frac{P_t}{P_{t-1}} - 1 \tag{5.44}$$

a definition of real wage rate

$$R_t = \frac{W_t}{P_t} \tag{5.45}$$

Constraints

[A]	$\delta \leq \delta^+$
[B]	$g \geq 0$
[C]	$N \leq L$
[D]	$R \geq R_{min}$
[E]	$i \geq 0$

(Variables)
endogenous variables:

$X, I, K, A, N, L, R, P, W, \delta, g, r', d, i, Z, \pi$

exogenous variables:

$\sigma, r^*, r^{**}, t, \epsilon, \beta_1, \beta_2, \gamma_1, \gamma_2, \pi^*, \theta, \Delta M, n, d_0, d_1$

$\omega_1, \omega_2, R^*, e^*, \nu, G_a, \delta^+, R_{min}, b_1, b_2$

The interest rate is determined by supply and demand in the bond market as formulated in eq.(5.38). The left side hand is the net supply of bond (flow) in the t-th period by government (including the central bank). And it is the sum of the part of bond issues in government deficit (θZ) and the net bond bought by government ($-\Delta M$). The demand for bond in private sector is both an increasing function of income and interest rate and a decreasing function of rate of profit. The increase of the rate of profit stimulates the investment and increases the supply of bond of funding. In summary, the rate of interest is both the increasing function of budget deficit and the rate of profit and the decreasing function of money supply and income. It can be specified as follows:

$$i_t = r'_t - b_1 \frac{X_t}{K_t} + b_2 \frac{\theta Z_t - \Delta M}{K_t} \tag{5.46}$$

We assume that the coefficient of the rate of profit is unity and $\Delta M/K_t$ is constant. Under the constraints ([A] - [D]) the movements of the model is the same as that of monopoly model. As to the constraint [E] i is supposed to be zero when the rate of interest becomes negative. From (5.30), (5.31), (5.33), (5.35) and (5.37), we obtain

$$r't = g_t + \frac{A_t}{K_t} - \sigma \delta_t t \tag{5.47}$$

Inserting Eq.(5.31) and (5.34), the above equation can be transformed as

$$r^* \delta_t^{1/\epsilon} = g_{t-1} + \beta_1(\delta_{t-1} - 1) + \beta_2 \left[b_1 \sigma \delta_t - b_2 \left\{ \theta \left(\frac{A_t}{K_t} - \sigma \delta_t t \right) - \frac{\Delta M}{K_t} \right\} - r^{**} \right] +$$

From this equation we can solve δ_t if $A_t/K_t, g_{t-1}, \delta_{t-1}$ are given. A_t/K_t can be solved by eq.(5.48), therefore, δ_t can be determined by pre-determined ((t-1)-the period) variables. If δ_t is determined, we can get r'_t, Z_t/K_t, $r'_t - i_t$, g_t and i_t in order.
From Eqs.(5.31), (5.33), (5.39), we can solve R_t and π_t;

$$\pi_t = \frac{R_{t-1}}{R_t} \frac{W_t}{W_{t-1}} - 1 \tag{5.48}$$

A_{t+1}/K_{t+1}, W_{t+1}/W_t and L_{t+1}/K_{t+1} are determined by Eqs. (5.36), (5.40), (5.41), (5.42) and (5.43).

5.3.3 Programs

```
10 '*****************
20 ' MONOPOLY MODEL
30 '*****************
40 PERIOD=100
50 DIM G(PERIOD),AK(PERIOD),LK(PERIOD),DEL(PERIOD),
R(PERIOD),PR(PERIOD),E(PERIOD),
D(PERIOD),WPAI(PERIOD)
60 '
70 '******* Parameter ********
80 SIG=.5 :NC=1 :BETA=.05
90 ES=.7 :GN=.05 :GA=.05
100 D0=.03 :D1=.1 :PRS=.25
110 EPS0=.7 :EPS1=.2 :W1=.1
120 W2=.1 :RS=.8
130 '
140 '********* Equilibrium *********
150 EQLK=NC * SIG/ES
160 EQR=(1 - PRS/SIG)/NC
170 EQD=D0+D1*EQR
180 EQG=GA+EQD
190 EQAK=PRS - EQG
200 EQWPAI=W1*(1 - EQR/RS)
210 '
220 RMIN=.01*EQR
230 DELMAX=((1 - RMIN * NC) * SIG/PRS) ∧ ((EPS0 -
EPS1)/(1 - EPS0+EPS1))
240 PRMAX=(1 - RMIN * NC) * SIG * DELMAX
250 '
260 '********* Initial Value *********
270 G0=.95 :AK0=1.15 :LK0=1.15:WPAI0=1.15
280 G(0)=G0 * EQG :AK(0)=AK0*EQAK:LK(0)=LK0*EQLK:
WPAI(T)=WPAI0*EQWPAI
290 GOSUB 420
300 '
310 '********* Computation ********
```

```
320 FOR T=1 TO PERIOD
330 G(T)=G(T - 1)+ BETA * (DEL(T - 1) - 1):
IF G(T)<0 THEN G(T)=0
340 AK(T)=AK(T - 1) * (1+GA)/(1+G(T - 1) - D(T - 1))
350 LK(T)=LK(T - 1) * (1+GN)/(1+G(T - 1) - D(T - 1))
360 WPAI(T)=W1*(1 - R(T - 1)/RS)+W2*(E(T - 1) - ES)
370 GOSUB 420
380 NEXT T
390 GOSUB 700
400 END
410 '
420 PR(T)=G(T)+AK(T)
430 GOSUB *DEL
440 R(T)=(1 - PR(T)/SIG/DEL(T))/NC
450 DELFULL=LK(T)/NC/SIG
460 IF DEL(T)<=DELMAX AND DEL(T)<=DELFULL THEN
GOTO 600
470 IF DELMAX > DELFULL THEN GOTO 520
480 R(T)=RMIN
490 DEL(T)=DELMAX
500 PR(T)=PRMAX :GOTO 580
510 '
520 DEL(T)=DELFULL
530 R(T)=(1 - PR(T)/SIG/DEL(T))/NC
540 IF R(T)> RMIN THEN GOTO 600
550 R(T)=RMIN
560 PR(T)=(1 - R(T)*NC)*DEL(T)*SIG
570 '
580 IF G(T)>PR(T) THEN G(T)=PR(T) :GOTO 600
590 '
600 E(T)=NC * SIG * DEL(T)/LK(T)
610 D(T)=D0+D1*R(T)
620 RETURN
630 '
640 *DEL
650 IF PR(T)>PRS THEN DEL(T)=(PR(T)/PRS) ∧ (EPS0 -
```

```
EPS1):RETURN
660 IF PR(T)<PRS THEN DEL(T)=(PR(T)/PRS) ∧ (EPS0+
EPS1):RETURN
670 DEL(T)=(PR(T)/PRS) ∧ EPS0
680 RETURN
690 '
700 PRINT TAB(7)"G"; TAB(14)"AK"; TAB(20)"LK"; TAB(28)"DEL";
TAB(35)"R"; TAB(42)"PR"; TAB(49)"E"; TAB(56)"D";
TAB(63)"WPAI"
710 FOR T=1 TO PERIOD
720 PRINT USING"###"; T; :PRINT USING"###.###"; G(T),
AK(T),LK(T),DEL(T),R(T),PR(T),E(T),D(T),WPAI(T)
730 NEXT T
740 RETURN
```

```
10 '*****************************
20 ' GOVERNMENT INTERVENTION MODEL
30 '*****************************
40 PERIOD=100
50 DIM G(PERIOD),AK(PERIOD),LK(PERIOD),DEL(PERIOD),
R(PERIOD),PR(PERIOD),E(PERIOD),D(PERIOD),
WPAI(PERIOD),ZK(PERIOD),IR(PERIOD)
PAI(PERIOD),PRICE(PERIOD),WAGE(PERIOD)
60 '
70 '******* Parameter ********
80 SIG=.5 : NC=.5 : BETA1=.15
90 BETA2=.005 : ES=.8 : GN=.03
100 ALPHA=.1 : D0=.08 : D1=.05
110 PRS=.2 : EPS0=.7 : EPS1=.2
120 W1=.01 : W2=.5 : RS=1.5
130 TX=.2 : GAMMA1=.1 : GAMMA2=.1
140 PAIS=.1 : THETA=.9 : I0=.001
150 I1=1 : IRS=PRS*.5
160 '
170 '********* Equilibrium *************
180 EQDEL=1
190 EQWPAI=PAIS
200 EQG=GN
210 EQR=(1 - PRS/SIG/(1 - TX))/NC
220 EQPRICE=1/EQR
230 EQD=D0+D1*EQR
240 EQAK=PRS - GS+TX*SIG
250 EQE=(EQPAI - W1*(1 - EQR/RS))/W2+ES
260 EQLK=NC*SIG/EQE
270 RMIN=EQR*.01
280 DELMAX=((1 - RMIN*NC)*SIG*(1 - TX)/PRS)^
((EPS0 - EPS1)/(1 - EPS0+EPS1))
290 PRMAX=(1 - RMIN*NC)*SIG*(1 - TX)*DELMAX
300 '
310 '******* Initial Value ***********
320 G1=.95 : AK1=1.15 : WK1=1.15 : WPAI1=1.15
```

```
330 G(1)=G1*EQG : AK(1)=AK1*EQAK : LK(1)=LK1*EQLK:
WPAI(1)=WPAI1*EQWPAI : WAGE(0)=1 : E(0)=EQE : R(0)=EQR
: PRICE(0)=WAGE(0)/R(0)
340 T=1 : GOSUB 480
350 '
360 '******** Computation ***********
370 FOR T=2 TO PERIOD
380 G(T)=G(T - 1)+BETA1*(DEL(T - 1) - 1)+BETA2*
(IRS - IR(T - 1)) : IF G(T)<0 THEN G(T)=0
390 IF DEL(T - 1)>=1 THEN LAMDA= - 1 ELSE LAMDA=1
400 AK(T)=AK(T - 1)+LAMDA*GAMMA1*(DEL(T - 1) - 1)^2
+GAMMA2*(PAIS - PAI(T - 1))
410 IF AK(T)<0 THEN AK(T)=0
420 LK(T)=LK(T - 1)*(1+GN)/(1+G(T - 1) - D(T - 1))
430 GOSUB 480
440 NEXT T
450 GOSUB 940
460 END
470 '
480 GOSUB *PR
490 PR(T)=PR
500 DEL(T)=(PR(T)/PRS)^EPS
510 R(T)=(1 - PR(T)/SIG/DEL(T)/(1 - TX))/NC
520 DELFULL=LK(T)/NC/SIG
530 IF DEL(T)<=DELMAX AND DEL(T)<=DELFULL THEN
GOTO 670
540 IF DELMAX > DELFULL THEN GOTO 580
550 R(T)=RMIN
560 DEL(T)=DELMAX
570 PR(T)=PRMAX : GOTO 650
580 '
590 DEL(T)=DELFULL
600 R(T)=(1 - PR(T)/SIG/DEL(T)/(1 - TX))/NC
610 IF R(T)> RMIN THEN GOTO 670
620 R(T)=RMIN
630 PR(T)=(1 - R(T)*NC)*DEL(T)*SIG*(1 - TX)
```

```
640 '
650 IF G(T)>PR(T)+SIG*DEL(T)*TX THEN
G(T)=PR(T)+SIG*DEL(T)*TX : GOTO 670
660 '
670 E(T)=NC*SIG*DEL(T)/LK(T)
680 D(T)=D0+D1*R(T)
690 ZK(T)=AK(T) - SIG*DEL(T)*TX
700 IR(T)=I0+I1*(THETA*ZK(T) - ALPHA)/SIG/DEL(T) :
IF IR(T)<0 THEN IR(T)=0
710 WPAI(T)=W1*(1 - R(T - 1)/RS)+W2*(E(T - 1) - ES)
720 WAGE(T)=WAGE(T - 1)*(1+WPAI(T))
730 PRICE(T)=WAGE(T)/R(T)
740 PAI(T)=PRICE(T)/PRICE(T - 1) - 1
750 RETURN
760 '
770 *PR
780 A1=G(T)+AK(T)
790 GOSUB *ESP
800 DEF FNPR(PR)=PR+TX*SIG*(PR/PRS)∧EPS - A1
810 MAXPR=100 : MINPR=0
820 PR=(MAXPR+MINPR)/2
830 DIF=FNPR(PR)
840 IF ABS(DIF)<=.00001 THEN RETURN
850 IF DIF>0 THEN MAXPR=PR : GOTO 820
860 IF DIF<0 THEN MINPR=PR : GOTO 820
870 '
880 *ESP
890 IF G(T)+AK(T)>PRS+SIG*TX THEN EPS=EPS0 - EPS1:
RETURN
900 IF G(T)+AK(T)<PRS+SIG*TX THEN EPS=EPS0+EPS1:
RETURN
910 EPS=ESP0
920 RETURN
930 '
940 PRINT TAB(7)"G"; TAB(14)"AK"; TAB(20)"LK";
TAB(28)"DEL"; TAB(35)"R"; TAB(42)"PR"; TAB(49)"E";
```

```
TAB(56)"D"; TAB(63)"WPAI"
950 FOR T=1 TO PERIOD
960 PRINT USING"###"; T; : PRINT USING"###.###";
G(T),AK(T),LK(T),DEL(T),R(T),PR(T),
E(T),D(T),WPAI(T)
970 NEXT T
980 PRINT TAB(7)"ZK"; TAB(14)"IR"; TAB(20)"PAI";
TAB(28)"PRICE"; TAB(35)"WAGE"
990 FOR T=1 TO PERIOD
1000 PRINT USING"###"; T; : PRINT USING"###.###";
ZK(T),IR(T),PAI(T),PRICE(T),WAGE(T)
1010 NEXT T
1020 RETURN
```

References

Adachi,H., 1982, *Theory of Economic fluctuation* , Tokyo: Nihon Keizai Shimbun (in Japanese).

Aiba,Y., 1986, 'Production Period and Business Cycle – A Hayekian Model of Trade Cycle,' *Review of Economics*, Nihon Fukushi University, No.68 (in Japanese).

Bleaney,M.F., 1976, *Underconsumption Theories – A History and Critical Analysis*, New York: International Publishers.

Dobb,M., 1937, *Political Economy and Capitalism,* London: Routledge & Kegan Paul Ltd.

Dusenbery,J.S., 1968, *Business Cycles and Economic Growth*, New York: McGrow-Hill.

Frank,R., 1987, *Production Prices and Dynamical Process of the Gravitation of Market prices*, Frankfurt am Main: Verlag Peter Lang.

Frisch,R., 1933, 'Propagation Problems and Impulse Problems in Dynamic Economics,' in *Economic Essays in Honor of Gustav Cassel*, Allen & Unwin.

Goodwin,R.M., 1967, 'A growth cycle,' in C.H.Feinstein (ed.), *Socialism, Capitalism and Economic Growth*, Cambridge: Cambridge University Press.

Hagiwara,T., 1983, 'Comparative Dynamic Analysis of Trade Cycles – The Behavior of Firms, and Period and Amplitude of Cycles,' *Rokkodai Ronsyu*, Kobe University, January. (in Japanese)

Harberler,G., 1952, *Prosperity and Depression*, United Nations, 3rd ed.

Harrod,R.F., 1936, *The Trade Cycle: An Essay*, Clarendon Press.

Harrod,R.F., 1948, *Towards a Dynamic Economics*, London: Macmillan.

Harrod,R.F., 1973, *Economic Dynamics*, London: Macmillan.

Hayek,F.A.von, 1931, *Price and Production*, London: Routledge & Kegan Paul.

Hayek,F.A.von, 1933, *Monetary Theory and the Trade Cycle*, London: Jonathan Cape.

Hayek,F.A.von, 1939, *Profits, Interest and Investment*, London: Routledge & Kegan Paul.

Hicks,J.R., 1950, *A Contribution to the Theory of the Trade Cycle*, Oxford: Oxford University Press.

Hilferding,R., 1910, *Finance Capital: A study of the Latest Phase of Capitalist Development*, London: Routledge & Kegan Paul, [1981].

Itoh,M., 1988, *The Basic Theory of Capitalism: the Forms and Substance of the Capitalist Economy*, London: Macmillan.

Itoh,M., 1980, *Value and Crisis: Essays on Marxian Economics in Japan*, New York and London: Monthly Review Press.

Kaldor,N., 1940, 'A Model of Trade Cycle,' *Economic Journal*, Vol.50, No.197, March.

Kalecki,M., 1935, 'A Macrodynamic Theory of Business Cycles,' *Econometrica*, Vol.3, No.3, July.

Kalecki,M., 1954, *Theory of Economic Dynamics*, New York: Augustus M.Kelly Publishers.

Keynes,J.M., 1936, *The General Theory of Employment, Interest and Money*, London: Macmillan.

Kim,K., 1988, *Equilibrium Business Cycle Theory in Historical Perspective*, Cambridge: Cambridge University Press.

Kitano,M., 1977, 'A Model of Business Cycle,' *Ritsumeikan Economics*, Ritsumeikan Univ., Vol.26, No.5, Dec. (In Japanese).

Kitano,M., 1977, 'A Model of Trade Cycle,' *Ritsumeikan Economics*, Ritsumeikan Univ., Vol.26, No.5. (in Japanese).

Kitano,M., 1979, 'A Comparative Dynamics of Business Cycle,' *Ritsumeikan Economics*, Ritsumeikan Univ., Vol.28, No.1, April. (In Japanese)

Kydland,F.E. and Prescott,E.C., 1982, 'Time to build and Aggregate Fluctuations,' *Econometrica*, Vol.50.

Lenin,V.I., 1965, *Imperialism, the Highest Stage of Capitalism*, Peking: Foreign Languages Press.

Lucas,R.E., 1975, 'An Equilibrium Model of the Business Cycle,' *Journal of Political Economy*, Vol.83.

Luxemburg,R., 1913, *Die Akkumulation of Kapitals.*

Malthus,T.R., 1820, *Principles of Political Economy Considered with a View to their Practical Application*, 1st ed. London: John Murray, 1820, Reprinted in part in D.Ricardo, *Notes on Malthus*, vol.2. *The Works and Correspondence of David Ricardo*, P.Sraffa, ed. Cambridge: Cambridge University Press, 1951.

Marx,K., 1867, *Capital*, Hormondsworth: Penguin, [1976].

Marx,K., 1885, *Capital*, Hormondsworth: Penguin, [1978].

Marx,K., 1894, *Capital*, Hormondsworth: Penguin, [1981].

Matthews,R.C.O., 1959, *The Trade Cycle*, Cambridge: Cambridge University Press.

Mino,K., 1977, 'On Cyclical Growth: a Harrodian approach,' Hiroshima Economic Review, Hiroshima University, Vol.1, No.1, July.

Mitchell,B.R. & P.Deane, 1971, *Abstract of British Historical Statistics.*

Mullineux,A.W., 1984, *The Business Cycle after Keynes: A Contemporary Analysis*, Brighton: Wheatsheaf Books Ltd., U.K. and New Jersey: Barnes & Noble books, U.S.A.

Nakatani,T., 1984, 'A Constraint of the Real Wage Rate and Upper Turning Point,' *Journal of Economics*, Kobe Univ., Vol.149, No.3, March (In Japanese).

Nakatani,T., 1986, 'Monopolistic Behavior and Trade Cycle,' *The Annals of Economic Studies*, Kobe University, No.33 (in Japanese).

Niisato,Y., 1987, 'Overproduction of Consumption goods Sector and Upper Turning Point,' *Economic Review of Toyama*, Toyama University, Vol.33, No.1, July (in Japanese).

Niisato,Y., 1986, 'Bottleneck of Production Goods and Upper Turning Point,' *Economic Review of Toyama*, Toyama University, Vol.33, No.1, July (In Japanese).

Ochi,T., 1987, 'On Turning point of trade cycles in a Two-sector Economy,' *Rokkodai Ronsyu*, Kobe university. (in Japanese)

Ochi,Y., 1987, 'Business Cycle in Tow Sector Model,' *Rokkobai Ronsyu*, Kobe Univ., Vol.34,No2, April.

Okishio,N., 1964, 'Unstability of Harrod=Dormar's Steady Growth, ' *Kobe University Economic Review*, 1967.

Okishio,N., 1976, *On Accumulation* (Chikusekiron), Tokyo: Chikuma. (in Japanese)

Okishio,N., 1977, *Contemporary Economics I*, Tokyo: Chikuma (in Japanese).

Okishio,N., 1987, *Marxian Economics*, Tokyo: Chikuma (in Japanese).

Okishio,N., 1980, *The Analysis of Contemporary Capitalism*, Tokyo: Iwanami (in Japanese).

Okishio,N, 1988, 'A turning point of Trade Cycle,'(Jouhou Tenkan no ichi keiki), *Journal of Economics*, Kobe University (in Japanese).

Okishio,N., 1988, 'On Marx's Reproduction Schema,' *Kobe University Economic Review*, 1988.

Okishio,N., 1988, *Contemporary Economics II*, Tokyo: Chikuma (in Japanese

Peacock & Wiseman, *The Growth of Public Expenditure in U.K.*

Robinson,J., 1956, *Accumulation of Capital*, London: Macmillan.

Robinson,J., 1979, *The Generalization of the General Theory and Other Essays*, 2nd ed., London: Macmillan Press Ltd.

Samuelson,P.A., 1939, 'Interaction between the multiplier analysis and the principle of acceleration,' *Review of Economics and Statistics*, Vol.31, May.

Sato,M., 1975, 'On Underconsumption Crisis,' *Economic Review*, Kansai Univ., Vol.25,No.2-3-4, November. (in Japanese)

Sato,M., 1975, 'A Possibility of Occurring Crisis by the slowdown of consumption sector,' *Review of Economics*, Kansai University. (in Japanese)

Sato,Y., 1985, 'Marx-Goodwin Growth Cycles in a Two Sector Economy,' *Zeitschrift für Nationalökonomie*, Vol.45, No.1.

Schumpeter,J.A., 1939, *Business Cycles: A Theoretical, Historical and Statistical Analysis of the Capitalist Process*, New York: McGraw-Hill, 2 vols.

Schumpeter,J.A., 1934, *The Theory of Economic Development*, Oxford: Oxford University Press.

Shultz & Harris, *American Public Finance*

Shima,T., 1963, *Theory of Public Finance (in Japanese)*, Tokyo: Iwanami.

Sismondi, J.C.L.S., 1819, *Nouveaux principes d'Econie politique.*

Slutzky,E., 1937, 'Summation of Random Causes as the Source of Cycle Process,' *Econometrica*, Vol.5, No.2, April.

Sweezy,P.M., 1942, *The Theory of Capitalist Development*, New York: Monthly Review Press.

Tugan-Baranowsky,M.von, 1901, *Studien zur Theorie und Geschichte der Hadelskriesen in England.*

Umada,T., 1986, 'Oligopoly and Business Cycle,' *Rokkodai Ronsyu*, Kobe Univ., Vol.33, No.1, May. (in Japanese)

Uno,K., 1976, *Theory of Crisis*(Kyokoron), Tokyo: Iwanami, revised ed (in Japanese).

Uno,K., 1980, *Principles of Political Economy: Theory of a Purely Capitalist Society*, Sussex: Harvester Press.

U.S. Department of Commerce, 1960, *Historical Statistics of the United States.*

U.S. National Resources Committee, *The Structure of the American Economy*, vol.I.

Yamada,Y., *Estimation of National Income in Japan (in Japanese).*

DYNAMISCHE WIRTSCHAFTSTHEORIE

Herausgegeben von Peter Flaschel und Michael Krüger

Band 1 Reiner Franke: Production Prices and Dynamical Processes of the Gravitation of Market Prices. 1987.

Band 2 Peter Flaschel / Michael Krüger (eds.): Recent Approaches to Economic Dynamics. Conference Volume (Bielefeld: 7-9th October, 1987). 1988.

Band 3 Richard M. Goodwin: Essays in Nonlinear Economic Dynamics. Collected Papers 1980-1987. 1988.

Band 4 Peter Skott: Kaldor's Growth And Distribution Theory. 1989.

Band 5 Jobst H. Thalenhorst: Die Zeitstruktur der Produktion als Ursache ökonomischer Dynamik. 1989.

Band 6 Volker Bieta: Strategische Möglichkeiten für die Gestaltung von Zentralbankpolitiken. Eine spieltheoretische Analyse. 1990.

Band 7 Dimitrios Malliaropulos: Euromärkte und nationale Finanzmärkte. Geldmenge, Zins und Wechselkurs einer Eurowährung. Eine theoretische und empirische Analyse des Euro-DM-Marktes. 1990.

Band 8 Thomas Lux: Keynesianische Stabilisierungspolitik in Neokeynesianischen Modellen. 1990.

Band 9 Torsten Vogt: Technischer Fortschritt und Preisentwicklung. 1991.

Band 10 Marco Wilke: Corporatism and the Stability of Capitalist Democracies. 1991.

Band 11 Ingrid Kubin: Market Prices and Natural Prices. A Study in the Theory of the Classical Process of Gravitation. 1991.

Band 12 Nobuo Okishio (ed.): Business Cycles. Theories and Numerical Simulation. 1992.

www.ingramcontent.com/pod-product-compliance
Ingram Content Group UK Ltd.
Pitfield, Milton Keynes, MK11 3LW, UK
UKHW020121290926
15471UKWH00003B/209

9 783631 444108